PENGUIN
COMPASS

THE INDIAN LUCK BOOK

Monisha Bharadwaj was raised in Bombay where she is now an acclaimed author and television producer. Her unparalleled knowledge of Indian lifestyle and culture imbues her writing with the essence of India. She is the author of nine books including *The Indian Spice Kitchen, Beauty Secrets of India,* and *India Style.*

THE
Indian
Luck
BOOK

monisha bharadwaj

PENGUIN
COMPASS

PENGUIN COMPASS
Published by the Penguin Group
Penguin Putnam Inc., 375 Hudson Street,
New York, New York 10014, U.S.A.
Penguin Books Ltd, 80 Strand,
London WC2R ORL, England
Penguin Books Australia Ltd, 250 Camberwell Road,
Camberwell, Victoria 3124, Australia
Penguin Books Canada Ltd, 10 Alcorn Avenue,
Toronto, Ontario, Canada M4V 3B2
Penguin Books India (P) Ltd, 11 Community Centre, Panchsheel Park,
New Delhi — 110 017, India
Penguin Books (N.Z.) Ltd, Cnr Rosedale and Airborne Roads, Albany,
Auckland, New Zealand
Penguin Books (South Africa) (Pty) Ltd, 24 Sturdee Avenue,
Rosebank, Johannesburg 2196, South Africa

Penguin Books Ltd, Registered Offices:
Harmondsworth, Middlesex, England

First published in Great Britain by Kyle Cathie Ltd 2001
Published in Penguin Compass 2003

10 9 8 7 6 5 4 3 2 1

Copyright © Monisha Bharadwaj, 2001
Photographs copyright © Donna Eaves, 2001
All rights reserved

Illustrations on pages 54, 55, 57, and 60 by Clare Curtis

Library of Congress Cataloging-in-Publication Data

Bharadwaj, Monisha.
The Indian luck book / Monisha Bharadwaj.
p. cm.
Includes bibliographical references and index.
ISBN 0 14 21.9618 5 (pbk.)
1. Fortune. 2. Fortune-telling—India. 3. Hindu symbolism.
4. Astrology and gems. I. Title.
BF1778 .B43   2003
133.3'0954—dc21   2002070350

Printed in Singapore

Luck Tools

"The sun has risen; my good fortune has dawned."
Rig-Veda (between 1500 and 900 B.C.)

What is luck?

A quiz contestant wins a million dollars on a television show, a bank teller suddenly finds himself promoted to the position of a manager, and a young woman sitting in a café is offered a chance of a lifetime to become a supermodel and earn the world's adulation and envy. What is it about such an incident that makes us stop and wonder? Does it happen simply because a person was in the right place at the right time, or is it the result of that person's innate characteristics? There is a saying in India that if only hard work were needed for success in life, a farmer would be king.

There is no doubt that in the countless situations we encounter each day, something other than mere physical or intellectual supremacy shapes each outcome; something that stretches beyond being at the right place at the right time, or beyond sheer hard work. It is an unknown force that seems to bring everything together in the correct mix so that a fortuitous and almost blessed situation emerges. It is this powerful but intangible entity that we call luck that leads to a sequence of events that seem unexplained and beyond our control. Luck is subject to chance; you may have it at a particular moment, or you may not. It is also an enigma and is often spoken of as fortune, fate, destiny, kismet, a fluke, a godsend, a windfall, or serendipity. No one has been able to say exactly what luck is, but a great many people will readily tell you that they would rather have luck on their side than not.

Contents

This book is for my lucky charms, my children Arrush and Saayli, and for my husband Nitish who makes me feel like the luckiest woman alive.

The need for faith

In ancient India the sounds of sea-conches, mountain breezes, and birdcalls were all thought to carry messages.

It is not without reason that we say that faith can move mountains; we wish on a falling star, throw coins into a wishing well, and, as children, fight over the wishbone at dinnertime—all in the hope of attracting a little good luck our way. If you do not believe in luck or in its effectiveness, then none of the lucky remedies that are contained in this book will work for you. One gemologist I interviewed said to me, "The way to see by faith is to close the eye of reason."

There is a fine line between believing in luck and being superstitious. Both work on the same principle of faith, but superstition exists in the realm of myth and hearsay, whereas luck seems to reside in the universe occupied by science, art, and experience. Life can be enriched by having faith in the power of good luck, but this faith can be diminished by the fearful asphyxiation of superstition.

In India, we have always believed in the power of the mind. A colloquial saying runs, "If you truly decide you want something, not even the sun can resist the power of this wish." All Indian festivals include the ritual of inviting good luck into your home and life through symbolism and the chanting of specific mantras. Even meditation that is intended to calm the soul focuses energy on positive thoughts and peace. Indians believe it is the creation of strong and positive desire, as well as appropriate action, that ensures the satisfaction of a wish or the success of a project. A large number of Indians will happily try a luck remedy because they have an unshakable belief in the power of the unknown.

There are many times in our lives when we seem to need a good measure of luck. Sometimes progress seems to have reached a bottleneck, and no amount of hard work will nudge it along. A sudden stroke of Providence, unexplained and infinitely elusive, sometimes presents the answer. This book contains some of the ancient secrets of India that can usher a bit of Providence our way. There are luck remedies to use when relationships need a boost, when career success seems elusive, when money is tight, when health and well-being seem to go into a downward spiral, or when stress and seemingly intractable problems are overwhelming.

The ancient wisdom of India is powerful and yet cautious. Much can be achieved through sustained concentration and wishful prayers, but the ancient texts also warn that there is a limit to the efficacy of luck tools. The advice contained in this book is not meant to override professional medical advice, and I sincerely urge my readers who are suffering from physical or emotional problems to seek professional help. Also, if you feel that any of the luck tools listed in this book aggravate your problem, please discontinue their use immediately. Indeed, these remedies should be used on an individual basis after a thorough check of one's mental and physical health. A book such as this one can provide only general suggestions, empowering readers to make positive changes in their own lives.

History of Indian luck

It is difficult to ascertain exactly when the practice of inviting luck into our lives began in India. The art of divination, in which the future is read through signs, has been practiced in India for centuries. Even in the Vedic period (c. 1500 B.C.) people read and interpreted portents, or prophetic signs. The meaning of lightning, rain, and dew was deciphered, and the sounds of conch shells, mountain breezes, and birdcalls seemed to carry their own secret messages; even moles, warts, and birthmarks on the body were believed to reveal a person's destiny.

Ancient Indians were fascinated by the unknown, and thinkers attempted to discover secrets not apparent to the human eye or imagination. A popular book on dream interpretation was the *Swapna-Chintamani* (*Dream Thought Gem*), written by Jagaddeva (c.1780 B.C.). Here, fortunes were told from shadows, leaping flames, and the sum of certain numbers. These practices became widespread in the Middle Ages, whereas palmistry, which people now set much store by, is comparatively modern in origin.

Another ancient art that still flourishes today is astrology. Indians still believe in its power, and however educated or rational a person might be, he or she will consult an astrologer from time to time. Astrology came to India from the west, probably from Mesopotamia. The Chaldaeans, the greatest mathematicians and astrologers, lived in Mesopotamia. Most modern scholars believe that the Chaldeans discovered the science of celestial divination or astronomy.

Another influential group were the sun-worshiping Magas, who are believed to have been descendants of the Mongolian and Syrian peoples. Their religious leaders, known as magi (the origin of the word "magic"), practiced sorcery, astrology, architecture, and medicine. Equipped with their powerful knowledge, the magi became high priests at the courts of ancient Indian kings; they are even mentioned in the great epics, such as the *Ramayana* (written between 350 B.C. and A.D. 250) and the *Mahabharata* (probably written c. A.D. 400).

The history of India dates back more than 5,000 years. During this time, several systems of fortune-telling have been developed, streamlined, and passed down the generations. Even today people have their horoscopes drawn up to use through life as a luck tool. Babies are named according to their horoscope alphabet, horoscopes are matched before a marriage is arranged, and decisions affecting health and career are similarly made. People also spell their names according to the tenets of numerology; they draw lucky symbols outside their homes to invite prosperity; they grow lucky plants in their garden and heed any messages contained in their dreams.

The evil eye

Indians also associate luck with another curious practice. There are many hundreds of Indian languages and dialects, and every one has a word for the "evil eye." Loosely translated, this is the ill will wished upon people by detractors jealous of their good fortune. "Good fortune" can mean anything, from healthy children to a beautiful home to a foreign vacation. It is believed that a jealous curse directed at an unsuspecting person has the power to revoke that individual's good fortune. The evil eye, people believe, also casts an ominous shadow over any luck a person may have over the course of his or her life. As a precautionary measure, it is quite common for mothers to perform a ritual to cancel any negative forces that surround their children. They hold a handful of mustard seeds over their children while making a wish, then pop the seeds in a pan over a high heat and throw them away. Figuratively, they have collected and blown to bits any ill luck that may have attached itself to their children. However bizarre this custom may sound, all Indians grew up with the ritual and follow it even today. Perhaps it is belief alone that ensures that the children do not succumb to accidents or ill health after being exposed to envious neighbors or acquaintances.

Positive thinking

This brings me to the biggest factor that invites luck into our lives, and that is the power of positive thinking. A happy soul filled with positive thoughts is sure to attract good luck. A peaceful mind sees potential in every situation, while a depressed person is blind to fortune and searches for it in the wrong places. Lastly, this is a special message to all my readers—

Never ever underestimate the power of a wish; if you wish for something consistently enough as well as deeply, it is bound to come true, making you feel like the luckiest person alive. I have had personal experience of this many times in my life. I almost feel that I can will a good thing to happen by pouring all my positive energy into a wish.

Traditional Indian tools for good luck

According to ancient Indian wisdom, various tools can bring good fortune into one's life when used correctly. Some of these are worn, some are spoken, and some are deciphered after much study and practice. Many of these tools are of scientific origin, but have acquired wider cultural significance through sustained and widespread use. All the tools listed here have withstood the test of time and are quite simple to use. They are still known and respected by Indians all over the world.

Gems

In India, gems are known as *ratna,* which means bestowed by god. Gems are among the richest fruits of the earth—lustrous, rare, and infinitely precious. Gemology is an ancient science, and historical evidence shows that it was practiced even in the first century B.C., one of the oldest recorded stones being amber. Rubies, amethysts, and corals, which were found soon after, were also worn with pride. Medieval Indian texts by the gemologists Buddhabhatta and Narayana-Pandit describe *ratna-pariksha* or gem study, and Hindu mythology is replete with stories of fabulous, celestial gems. The *Kurma Purana* (c. A.D. 900) as well as the *Garud Purana* (c. A.D. 1000), both Sanskrit texts rich with the lore of gods and goddesses, discuss the potency of gems worn for good luck.

One of the most fascinating stories in Indian mythology is that of the "Churning of the Ocean," in which gods and demons pulled on the two ends of a mythical snake called Vasuki in order to churn the Divine Ocean and thereby obtain the nectar of immortality. During this powerful churning, the ocean offered up prototypes of all the jewels known to man. In appreciation for the part played by Vasuki, certain gems were handed to the king of snakes, such as the *chintamani* (thought-jewel) and the *divya-ratna* (divine gem), both capable of granting wishes and bringing great luck. Even today, Indians believe that snakes are the guardians of hitherto undiscovered treasures.

How do gems work?

Gems are believed to have the power to increase vitality, counteract negative influences, safeguard health, prevent accidents and accelerate progress. However, gems cannot wholly alleviate problems. They can only act as shock absorbers, cushioning negativity. Most gems are found as minerals deep inside the earth's crust. In this state, they absorb energy for millions of years before being discovered. This electromagnetic energy is later released with good or bad effects. It is very important to know which gems suit an individual person or specific circumstance. A point to note here is that gems range from precious stones, such as rubies, emeralds, and diamonds to semiprecious stones, such as turquoise and garnet.

A birthstone is mostly worn as a personal gem, a cosmic bond between you and your birthday.

The primary way in which gems work is by correcting our color deficiencies. The human body is dependent on light and color to function properly. Light is required for healthy cell function, and each color absorbed into the body creates vibrations that sustain our very life force. Astrologers maintain that each planet governs a particular cosmic color and energy. At the time of our birth, some planets are farther away than others, and, as a result, we are each deficient in a planetary color and influence. Gems help compensate for these deficiencies and create equilibrium of energies. The darker the color of a stone, the more intense and physical its effects will be. On the other hand, a lighter-colored stone will have softer, more spiritual effects.

Birthstones

In astro-gemology, birthstones are linked to signs of the zodiac, and can be worn by people born under the same sign to enhance the positive qualities and abilities with which the sign is associated. Each month's birthstone is the same color as the planet farthest from Earth at that time. The art of gemology deals primarily with finding a stone to counteract a specific malady.

Chart of birthstones

(certified by the National Association of Jewelers, U.S.A., since 1912)

Month & zodiac sign	Planet	Luck birthstones
Aquarius (Jan 21–Feb 21)	Uranus/Saturn	hessonite
Pisces (Feb 22–Mar 21)	Jupiter/Neptune	cat's-eye
Aries (Mar 22–Apr 20)	Mars	ruby or red coral
Taurus (Apr 21–May 21)	Venus	diamond/white sapphire
Gemini (May 22–June 21)	Mercury	emerald
Cancer (June 22–July 22)	Moon	pearl
Leo (July 23–Aug 22)	Sun	ruby
Virgo (Aug 23–Sept 22)	Mercury	emerald
Libra (Sept 23–Oct 23)	Venus	diamond/white sapphire
Scorpio (Oct 24–Nov 21)	Mars	ruby/red coral
Sagittarius (Nov 22–Dec 21)	Jupiter	yellow sapphire
Capricorn (Dec 22–Jan 20)	Saturn	blue sapphire

How to buy a gem

Good-quality gemstones are available internationally, but in India every jeweler has a store of them, possibly because of the strength of belief Indian people have in gemology. When choosing a gem, it is important to keep the following points in mind.

types of stones It is important to know what kind of stone you are buying. Gems used for luck must be natural or simulant, as only these types possess the necessary properties.

Natural This is a mineral found in a rock within the earth.

Simulant This is also a natural stone, but is used in gemology as a replacement for a more expensive stone, for example, a citrine (simulant) is sometimes used as an alternative to the more expensive yellow sapphire. Both stones are yellow and resemble each other.

Synthetic This stone is manufactured in a laboratory but bears the same physical, chemical, and optical properties as a natural stone.

Man-made This is also crafted in a laboratory but does not have the properties of a real stone. An example of a man-made gem is the rhinestone.

Imitation Exactly what the name suggests, it is also called "glass," "plastic" or, in jewelers' terms, "paste."

carat weight

Gemology, or the science of gems, prescribes cures for personal problems, almost as a doctor prescribes medicines. The prescribed "dosage", which includes the carat weight of a gem, reflects the intensity of a client's problem. Gemologists prescribe a particular carat weight for each individual; however, they believe that, as in the Law of Diminishing Returns, it is rarely beneficial to wear a stone weighing over five carats. A weight higher than this will show only a minimal increase in results. When choosing a stone for a child, it is advisable to buy one that is under a carat in weight.

clarity In India, we are very particular about blemishes in stones, especially in diamonds, as we believe such flaws bring bad luck. Of course, in the case of transparent or translucent colored stones, it is rare to find a stone with no spot or feather (this looks almost like a hairline crack within the stone). You will find that the price of diamonds is proportional to their clarity.

testing It is easy for a novice buyer to be misled when buying a stone. There are endless varieties, and many resemble each other, while a cascade of glittering jewels can boggle the mind of the most hardened buyer. A relatively new synthethic stone is the moisonite, which is so similar in appearance to a diamond that it can fool an expert. Before purchasing a stone, the safest course is to have it professionally tested, for a small fee, by a reputable jeweler. Issued with a certificate of authenticity, you can enjoy your gem and peace of mind.

energizing your stone Gemologists claim that no stone will show any effect until is has been cleansed and energized. You can wear any stone as an ornament without cleaning and energizing it, but a luck stone must be "activated" to release the energy it has accumulated and stored over millennia and to remove any negative vibrations it picked up before reaching you. Although there are several procedures, the one outlined below is widely followed and held to give the best results:

After making the appropriate checks, set your stone into a ring or a pendant. Luck stones are almost always worn like this.

Identify the best day to first wear your stone (see below), and, on the night before, immerse it in a cup of fresh milk, which is sacred and naturally pure. Then place the cup before an image of your god, or something you hold in the highest regard, and leave it there overnight.

The next morning at dawn, rinse the stone, raise it to the rising sun — the most elevated form of energy — and pray to the forces of nature that your wish be granted through the stone. Start wearing it immediately.

The best day to start wearing your stone

Sunday	ruby
Monday	pearl
Tuesday	red coral
Wednesday	emerald
Thursday	yellow sapphire, cat's-eye
Friday	diamond
Saturday	blue sapphire

Color

Although it is difficult to change your favorite color to become the person you wish to be, you can wear different colors in situations where you feel a need for luck.

Humans have always been fascinated by color. In India, the effect of color on the human psyche was first appreciated thousands of years ago. People surrounded themselves with the bright colors that they associate with a divine nature. They believed that by creating an aura of color around themselves, they would attract the natural forces that bestow good fortune. They made dyes from materials at hand: turmeric and saffron gave yellow, the root and bark of the Indian mulberry gave a rich red, larkspur flowers gave a light yellow, and the native indigo plant gave blues and purples. A wide array of other natural ingredients, such as pomegranate rinds, cockscomb flowers, and henna leaves, were blended to create subtle shades and tints.

Nature itself offers millions of colors to feed the mind and the spirit. We all feel the vital energy of a blazing yellow sun, the calming effects of a cloudless, azure sky, and the feelings of renewal inspired by a jewel-green forest. This is because human beings are composed of color vibrations, and we respond consciously or subconsciously to color at every moment of our lives. Our growth, sleep, state of mind, and continued vitality are all governed by color. Color also draws certain kinds of negative and positive vibrations toward us. Of course, if you believe a color you favor will bring luck, you will yourself create circumstances that invite good fortune. Having said that, colors themselves promote good luck, as well as positive thinking. The use of color to promote physical and spiritual well-being is truly an art.

How does color work?

Throughout our lives, we are conditioned to block out certain emotions. These may be linked to diffidence, fear, full expression of joy, or pride or the display of sorrow. When blocked, these emotions can create an aura of pain and negativity around us. Indians believe that the energies affecting our bodies are in turn controlled by the chakras. These are focal points of psychic energy, and there are said to be eighty-eight thousand of them in the human body.

In Indian traditional medicine, the seven most important chakras are used in diagnosing ailments, both physical and emotional. Each is represented in color with a lotus at its center:

Muladhara chakra (at the base of the spine): golden chakra with pink lotus.

Swadhishtana chakra (in the small of the back): colorless chakra with vermilion lotus.

Manipura chakra (in the lumbar region): red chakra with blue lotus.

Anahata chakra (in the heart): flaming red chakra with golden lotus.

Vishuddha chakra (near the throat): gold chakra with smoky blue lotus.

Ajna chakra (between the eyebrows): white chakra with white lotus.

Sahasrara chakra (above the crown of the head): a mixture of all colors with a multicolored lotus.

In India, we believe that these chakras can absorb color from the external world, making the individual more balanced and happy. There are healing color remedies for various maladies and even "lucky" colors for each sign of the zodiac.

Healing colors for the signs of the zodiac

Zodiac Sign	Color	Remedy for
Aries	red	impatience
Taurus	green	laziness
Gemini	orange	indecision
Cancer	orange	insecurity
Leo	gold	withdrawn countenance
Virgo	apple green	criticizing nature
Libra	green	airiness
Scorpio	blue green	secretiveness
Sagittarius	blue	envy
Capricorn	deep blue	ruthless pursuit of duty
Aquarius	violet	oversensitivity
Pisces	red violet	low self-esteem

Indians also believe in instinctively felt lucky colors. For some reason, mine is lemon yellow. I have always believed that anything that I undertake while wearing this shade will be successful. Thus I own, and have worn, a variety of lemon yellow outfits to employment interviews, hospital checkups, and on trips abroad. In fact, according to the rules of color psychology, this is probably because the color yellow is associated with the ability to boost self-confidence and banish thoughts of fear or confrontation. In India, yellow is linked to the sun's energy, a vital force that infuses a person with radiance and power.

Indians have such a strong belief in the power of color that they use several color therapies, such as solar ray therapy, in which sunlight is filtered through colored glass for healing and luck. Homes are painted in vibrant hues, and gods are associated with lucky colors; Krishna is India's best-loved god and is always depicted as blue. The natural elements, especially revered in India, are also identified with colours: air, water, earth, fire, and space are silver, blue, brown, red, and white respectively, and these colors are used in clothing, food, and interiors to symbolize the elements.

Here are some of the common associations of color. Check your personality type against your favorite color:

Color	Personality
Red	sensual, angry, vital, assertive
Pink	calm, loving, very easygoing
Orange	warm, humorous, insufficiently diligent
Yellow	bright, intelligent, fearful of new situations
Green	peaceful, generous, self-controlled
Turquoise	youthful, confident, able to concentrate
Blue	relaxed, faithful, wise
Purple	flamboyant, mystical, creative
Magenta	flexible, considerate, spiritual
Black	lonely, confident, clear-thinking
White	pure, cold, insular
Gray	independent, self-analytical, passionate
Gold	forceful, ambitious, dramatic
Silver	sensitive, understated, fickle
Brown	nurturing, too easily satisfied, sedate.

❖ Symbols

The Hindu use of motifs and symbols is age-old, but it continues to be expressed through architecture, art, dress, literature, religion, and ritual. Symbols are considered lucky because of their color, shape, mystical ties, traditional usage, and the objects they signify. In particular, lucky symbols are associated with divinity and spirituality.

According to Indian mythology, the first lucky symbols were created during the Great Churning of the Divine Ocean, when gods and demons churned the mighty waters in order to find the nectar of immortality, also known as *amrit*. At first, there appeared a noxious, scum-like poison which was consumed by the powerful god Shiva. Then there appeared fourteen treasures that are considered extremely auspicious and lucky. They are represented by ancient Indian symbols of divinity; Indian symbolism attempts to bring the power of the Divine within the grasp of the devotee or mortal.

Chandra	the Moon
Parijata	a rich, fragrant tree
Airavat	a four-tusked elephant
Kamadhenu	a wish-fulfilling cow
Mada	the goddess of wine, who held a jeweled bowl of wine
Kalpavriksha	a wish-fulfilling, immortal tree
Rambha	a beautiful celestial nymph
Uchaishravas	an exquisite white horse that uttered mystic syllables
Lakshmi	the goddess of fortune and wealth
Shankha	the conch of victory
Gada	the mace of sovereignty
Dhanush	the bow of magic
Ratna	a cascade of gems
Dhanvantari	physician of the gods bearing the amrit
Amrit	the nectar of immortality in a golden *kumbha*, or chalice

How do symbols work?

All lucky symbols capture and convey the energy of the physical as well as spiritual world they represent. Thus they are drawn in front of homes, embroidered on to fabric, crafted into jewelery designs, painted on furniture and walls, or depicted on paper and carried in handbags and coin purses. People use symbols to protect all that they cherish, enhance their luck, promote their health, and increase their appreciation for the beauty of form, color, and shape.

Types of symbols

There are two main types of symbols in Hinduism: sound symbols and visual symbols.

sound symbols Most sound symbols are syllables, or mantras, which are chanted over and over again to create powerful vibrations that will invite good fortune. Chanting is highly significant in Hindu ritual, and even little children are taught to use it as a source of strength and concentration. Sound symbols are easy to say, and although some seem to have no obvious meaning, they contain profound wisdom. Some scholars believe that by repeating apparently meaningless but powerfully symbolic mantras, one can see beyond the physical world to the eternal nature of the Divine.

The foremost sound symbol said to favor luck and auspicious tidings is "om" or "aum" (pronounced as "oam"). This represents the elementary sound of the universe; the secret music of the planets, galaxies, and stars as they move to a predestined rhythm. Even as we say the word "aum," cosmic energy and power move through the yogic centers in our body into our environment, thereby creating an aura of divine peace. Meditation involves sitting quietly and comfortably with one's eyes closed, chanting the mantra until it resonates within the mind and spirit.

Other sound symbols are called *bijaksharas*, or seeds of syllables that have mystical vibrations when uttered. Some of these *bijaksharas*, "aim," "hrim," "klim" etc., are apparently without meaning but have the power to protect us from harm, sharpen our faculties, and calm our senses.

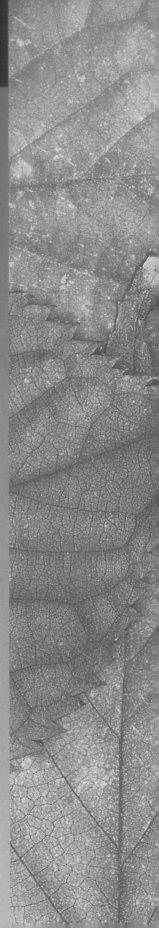

visual symbols Around 1500 B.C., when the Vedas, or the four great books of knowledge, were created to represent the universe and its cosmic energy, some visual symbols were used as a focus of meditation, while others were used in ritual and worship. Visual symbols can be divided into natural shapes and spiritual or geometrical shapes.

Natural shapes There are innumerable lucky symbols inspired by fruits, flowers, trees, animals, and other natural objects. Prime among these is the lotus. This beautiful flower is depicted in many forms and used extensively in temple architecture. For example, gods and goddesses appear seated in a pink or white lotus.

The lotus stands for grace and beauty, operating as an example of how men and women should lead their lives. In nature, the lotus grows in brackish pools crowded with weeds and moss, but it stands apart, complete in its beauty and oblivious to its murky surroundings. This is a state we should emulate, irrespective of the mundane or turbulent world around us.

The lotus also signifies knowledge and good fortune. It is closely associated with the goddess Lakshmi, who is the deity of wealth and luck. The many petals of the lotus symbolize the layers of the human personality; just as the petals open, the individual attains spirituality and self-awareness. The heart of the lotus represents release from earthly bondage with eternal bliss thereafter.

The image of a lotus and a hovering bee is repeatedly used in devotional literature in order to portray the Divine as a beautiful, fragrant flower, with the devotee being the bee irresistibly attracted to it.

Other natural symbols include snakes, the coconut, a pot full of water, footprints of the goddess Lakshmi, the Sun, the Moon, the tortoise, the conch, elephants, swans, and deer.

Spiritual or geometrical shapes These are usually diagrams bound by a circle that contains squares, triangles, and crystalline or stellar patterns within it. These symbols have been used in India for thousands of years and more recently by Jungian psychologists to symbolize the structure of the human psyche. These geometric symbols, called *mandalas,* are said to be concentrated centers of psychic energy, enclosed and guarded by the power of the universe. The best known *mandala* is the *srichakra*, a potent symbol which is the essence of enclosed psychic vibrations. It represents the elements, such as fire, air, water, earth, and space; the elementals, such as wind, cold, heat, rain; all the Hindu deities; the entire phonetic system; the yogic chakras, and Shiva and Shakti, which represent matter and energy. Thus, this *yantra*, or symbol, holds the entire universe and its power. At its geometric heart is a dot, or *bindu*, which symbolizes a potential burst of sound and movement and is almost a seed of the cosmic universe. Three triangles around this core signify the three worlds of heaven, earth, and hell; the three human states of waking, dream, and sleep; the past, present, and future; and the three personality types: *satva* (calm and saintly), *rajas* (royal, fond of pleasures), and *tamas* (baser instincts).

Many symbols are based on the principle that we create the meaning of experience. After all, there are as many meanings of the word "life" as there are people in the world! Symbols serve as tools for constructing belief.

✦ Metals

Mining and metalwork were practiced in ancient India. Gold, silver, and bronze were popular even before the Vedic period, and soon afterwards tin (1500 B.C.) and iron (900 B.C.) were discovered. There is evidence that steel was used by 500 B.C. and brass a few hundred years later. Early Sanskrit texts such as *Arthashastra* (written between 391 and 296 B.C.) and the ayurvedic works of Charaka (c. A.D. 80–180) also mention the use of metals. Of all known metals, five were believed to be of special significance. These were gold, silver, copper, bronze, and iron, collectively known as *pancha-dhatu.*

gold is known as *suvarna*, which has a variety of meanings, such as "beautiful colour" and "heavenly." Gold is considered precious and pure because it does not rust or tarnish. It was dubbed the king of metals and believed to be a fragment of the sun—lustrous, beautiful, and eternal. Gold is still considered the most auspicious metal and is used to decorate gods and goddesses, temples, and altars. Anyone who wears gold is destined to enjoy good fortune. However, the gold has to be as pure as possible. That is why all Indians believe in wearing no less than twenty-two-carat pure gold. Twenty-four carat gold, the purest gold, is sometimes used in jewelery, but is so soft that it does not have the strength to hold its shape. Indians do not believe that fourteen or eighteen carat gold possesses any auspicious properties. Gold is thought to be so sacred that Indians will not wear jewelery made of pure gold on their feet, as to do so would be disrespectful and equal to inviting the ire of Lakshmi, the goddess of wealth and luck. Only the divine deities can wear this beautiful metal as anklets or toe rings, which makes them appear even more enchanting!

silver, or *rupya*, meaning of "beautiful appearance," was regarded as a slice of the moon. It is still considered especially sacred, and idols of gods and goddesses, as well as utensils used in ancient ritual and religious ceremony, are all made of silver.

copper was revered because of its warm glow and known medicinal properties, and some utensils used in traditional worship were fashioned from this metal. Today copper is still used for health luck and in cures for specific ailments.

bronze was used for making statues of deities, with a little gold or silver added for extra good luck. Bell metal, which resembles brass, was used for

How do metals work?

Since ancient times, the smelting of metal with fire and the casting of metal objects have been endowed with mystery. In some societies, a blacksmith was seen as a shaman who could read the messages and fortunes of different worlds, and he was respected for his extraordinary powers. In India, the intrinsic properties of metals are linked with the planets. When we wear a metal next to our skin, its chemical properties interact with our physical being, bringing the heavenly bodies into direct contact with our lives and affecting the way we feel.

Gold is associated with the sun because of its physical attributes, but it also contains the energy of Mars, namely purity and the ability to purify everything it touches. Silver has an affinity with the moon, sharing its artistic temperament, and wearers of silver are more likely to be influenced by gentle lunar energy. Copper is governed by the Sun and shares its healing properties. It was once considered magical, due to its strange glow, and was used in the worship of the mother goddess, who possessed extraordinary, supernatural powers. The metal of Saturn, iron is believed to help alleviate negative feelings and encourage fruitfulness of action. The Iron Pillar of Mehrauli, made in A.D. 325 of a single piece of iron, still stands today, powerful and strong. The planet Mercury governs the metal lead, which encourages prudence and discretion.

Vastu Shastra

Indians are meticulous housekeepers and consider their homes to be temples for the body and spirit—places where mind and body can be cleansed and nourished.

Indians' reverence of the home finds expression in Vastu Shastra ("vastu" meaning environment or structure and "shastra" meaning science). This ancient science encompasses the fields of design, engineering, earth science, astronomy, and mystic sciences. When formulating its fundamental principles, ancient Indian sages considered the five elements in nature—earth, fire, water, air, and space—as well as the influence of the planets. Vastu Shastra was intended to create balance and harmony between man, his natural environment, and his home, enhancing happiness and good luck. It emphasizes the role of the five elements within a house: fresh air promotes health; water signifies movement and fluidity; fire purifies; earth represents energy and fecundity; and space resonates with the Divine. Unlike the Chinese science of feng shui, Vastu Shastra does not suggest that arrangement of objects promotes luck. Instead, it prescirbes the orientation of specific rooms and features.

The science of Vastu Shastra is complemented by certain customs followed in every Hindu home. Vastu Shastra stipulates that every house must have a threshold. In addition, Indians customarily remove their footwear at an entrance. They also paint auspicious designs, or *rangoli*, around their thresholds. Rice flour is sprinkled on the floor to create lucky symbols and motifs, such as parrots, peacocks, flowers, and leaves. Moreover, when a bride enters her new home, she overturns a cup of rice, to signify the luck and plenty she brings with her. Another principle of Vastu Shastra is that the home is a theater of light and air. This is why people allow the rays of the rising sun into their eastern rooms and light oil lamps in each room at dusk. The gentle fragrance of sandalwood, musk, or rose fills the air of a Hindu home as incense is burned each day to perfume, purify, and sanctify the space.

How does Vastu Shastra work?

Vastu Shastra prescribes the direction and decoration of specific rooms and architectural features so that the beneficial effects of the five elements are felt within the home, leading in turn to health, prosperity, and luck. Its rules work in harmony with astrology. Firstly, it suggests ideal color schemes for the home and office, depending on one's zodiac sign, which bring luck and prosperity. Secondly, it teaches that each direction is governed by a planet, which is identified with a color, and that this color brings luck when used in conjunction with the corresponding direction.

Vastu Shastra suggests ideal color schemes for each sign of the zodiac:

Aquarius	blue, pink, cream
Pisces	sparkling white, yellow
Aries	coral red
Taurus	milky white
Gemini	green
Cancer	rose, pearl white
Leo	off-white, ruby red
Virgo	various soft colors
Libra	milky white, yellowish white
Scorpio	coral red, pink
Sagittarius	golden yellow
Capricorn	dull red, yellowish white

The exterior of a building can be painted according to the governing planet of the direction it faces:

East	Sun	brilliant white
West	Saturn	blue
North	Mercury	green
South	Mars	coral red, pink
Northeast	Jupiter	golden yellow
Southwest	Mercury	green
Southeast	Venus	silvery white
Northwest	Moon	white, light yellow

Every home must have an area for worship or meditation, where positive thoughts can be focused and concentrated, so that good luck will be invited into one's home and life. Whether this is a small temple, altar, or any other place, it is essential to actively worship or pray there, so that good energies are drawn into one's environment.

The five elements in our home

The Vastu Shastra compares a house to the human body, with the front door representing the mouth. Just as we should eat food that is not only filling but also nutritious, so should we suffuse our homes with good and noble thoughts. As the body processes food and finally removes waste from the rear, so the home should have smaller doors within and a rear door in line with the front door for the disposal of evil energies that remain in the home.

The concept of opening a door to welcome in the good that waits on the other side is at the heart of Indian philosophy. It is the reason why temple doors are ceremonially opened each morning to reveal the bejeweled deity within. The main door therefore must necessarily be the largest door in the home, so that it will invite good luck from outside into the home.

Numbers

Numbers have played a significant role in Hindu occultism and astrology since ancient times. Sages and seers studied the mysterious realm of numbers, their relationship with the planets, and their effect on human life. Although the cultural importance of numbers has its roots in Babylon and China, their value was also stressed in ancient Indian mythological and mystical writings. In early times, certain numbers were believed to have magical properties. By the Middle Ages this belief had evolved into the science of numerology. The numbers believed to be most powerful were:

0   the symbol of *shunya*, or nothingness, which is still considered to be extremely powerful. It is nothing and yet contains the presence of everything within its continuous circle.

1   the number of the divinity of light and the sun of wisdom

2   the number of the moon

3   the special number of the triad, the perfect triangle

5   the number of measure—for example, the senses or fingers

9   the number signifying the nine orifices of the body, so a very physical number

17   a mystical number of sanctification and purity

108   another mystical number comprising the planets, the zodiac, constellations, and several heavenly bodies. There are said to be 108 special shrines in India, 108 beads in a Hindu rosary, and 108 poses of Nataraja, the Hindu god of dance, who in Indian mythology is said to balance the universe with his cosmic movements.

Although ancient Hindu researchers delved into the mystery of numbers, they also endeavored to hide their secrets from the common people. As a consequence, we know their results but have lost their original formulas.

How does numerology work?

Numerology forewarns of impending hardships so that one can meet challenges and correct imbalances. It is closely linked to astrology, and with its help, one can forecast a person's future by calculating the influence of the numbers peculiar to his or her date and time of birth. This is done by correlating numbers with planets to enforce the synergies that exist between them. Each number corresponds to a planet:

Sun	1	Moon	2
Jupiter	3	Uranus	4
Mercury	5	Venus	6
Neptune	7	Saturn	8
Mars	9		

How to find your number

There are four types of personal numbers, and each one is calculated very simply.

Birth number This is the single number derived from the sum of the birth date. For example, a person born on the twenty-seventh of a month will have a birth number of nine (2 + 7 = 9).

Spiritual number Also called the date of birth number or conscience number, this is the single digit derived from the sum of the entire birth date, which includes the day, month, and year. For example, a person born on the twenty-seventh of November 1970 will have a spiritual number of one (2 + 7 + 1 + 1 + 1 + 9 + 7 + 0 = 28; 2 + 8 = 10; 1 + 0 = 1).

Name number This is the number that corresponds to the letters in one's first and last names. Although there are several systems for assigning numbers to letters, this is the most popular:

A – 1	F – 8	K – 2	P – 8	U – 6	Z – 7
B – 2	G – 3	L – 3	Q – 1	V – 6	
C – 3	H – 5	M – 4	R – 2	W – 6	
D – 4	I – 1	N – 5	S – 3	X – 5	
E – 5	J – 1	O – 7	T – 4	Y – 1	

The highest of the basic numbers is nine. This is the number of divinity, and it is not assigned to any single letter. A Hindu rosary is made up of 108 beads (nine in numerological terms) and is said to reveal the rhythm of time and space while allowing the mind to concentrate on divinity.

Year number This is the single number that results from adding the digits of a birth year. For example, $1 + 9 + 7 + 0 = 17$ then $1 + 7 = 8$. Experience shows that years in numerical harmony with one's birth year are more eventful. If you simply add the digits of your birth year, you will find that past years with the same numerological value have been lucky. You can also prepare for yourself a cyclic chart of good-luck years to come.

Each numerological system provides different information about ourselves. The spiritual number reveals the basic personality traits we are born with. The name number relates to one's occupation and social status. The year number provides an indication of major events that will occur in the future. However, from the numerological point of view, the birth number is the most important . For example, numerologists try to match the birth number with the name number to create positive vibrations and promote good luck.

Dreams

Mythology and history are peppered with instances of dream prophecy in which people have conversed with higher spirits, seen incidents, or felt emotions through their dreams.

Dreams have always been significant in Hindu metaphysics because they provide a means of understanding the world around us. Hindu philosophical writings describe various states of wakefulness. In the waking state we are least able to perceive truth. As we live out our lives on earth, we are surrounded by a web of illusion. *Maya*, or illusion, refers to the physical world in which everything is transitory and not what it seems. The spiritual world, which is inhabited by the soul, is the realm of certainty and truth, and it is most clearly perceived in our dreams.

Dreams have been used for divination for thousands of years, although systems of interpretation have varied. Hindu thought subscribes to several schools of dream psychology. In Nyaya theory, dreams are representative—that is, the recollection of past physical experience in a subconscious state. The physician Charaka (second century A.D.), who was the father of the Ayurvedic system of medicine, claimed that dreams were both prophecies and the subconscious fulfilment of desires, while another great physician, Sushruta (fourth century A.D.), used the symbolism in dreams to diagnose illnesses.

Contemporary research shows that telepathy does occur and that during sleep, thoughts and ideas can be conveyed across a distance of many miles. Similarly, the dreaming mind is often influenced by the waking mind. When the waking mind is occupied by a particular situation or problem, the dreaming mind can offer a solution. The waking mind, overcome by events, is a barometer of the past, while the dreaming or spiritual mind, forever seeking answers, is a barometer of the future. Thus in a unique symbiotic exchange, our waking life contributes to our spiritual development and our inner knowledge plays a part in enriching our material life.

How can we use dreams?

When we are awake, our mind turns to logic and reason. In dreaming, we use our intuition to decipher invisible signs or influences. It is possible to harness the spiritual messages contained in our dreams to guide our destiny, instead of allowing ourselves to be controlled by it. For example, a man may hear the sound of a delivery van, but he cannot tell by the mere sound of the wheels what it contains. It is only when he sees the van that he fully understands its purpose. It is the same with symbols contained in dreams; we recognize them fully only when we see them in relation to our physical life.

All dreams deliver messages. However, few of us believe in the potency of dreams, and fewer still are able to decipher the messages contained in their dreams. If we learn to read between the lines of our dreams, we will be able to influence our destiny in a more deliberate and positive way. Dreams do not offer clear and explicit predictions, but they do give impressions of the future and help us to draw lessons from the past and the present.

How to develop the power to dream

Researchers have found that women dream more often and more intensely than men, because they are generally more aware of their emotional state. The first step to willful dreaming is to go to bed in a calm state and concentrate on the question troubling you. This takes practice, but you will soon find that the dreaming mind works in harmony with your wakeful mind, providing helpful answers to present and future dilemmas. A clue to the connection between the soul and the future is that it is not uncommon to dream of something during the night and to see it in the physical world the following day.

We rarely dream the same dream twice unless it is a recurring nightmare. This is because our own spiritual receptivity fluctuates from time to time, and our perceptions about a situation also vary at different times in our lives. Similarly, it is because our physical and spiritual states are not in perfect harmony with each other that we forget our dreams. Keep a pen and paper at your bedside, and write down your dreams on waking. You may have several dreams in one night. Note down as many as you can remember, and see if they bear a relationship to each other. Dreams are voices from a faraway realm, as real and as potent as a true friend sitting right by your side.

Some common dreams and their meanings

Anxiety This is usually a good omen suggesting a rejuvenation of the mind after a disturbing state.

Blood When on your hands, it denotes immediate bad luck, so be careful. Bloodstained clothes represent enemies waiting to demolish your blossoming career.

Crying To dream of someone else crying denotes a happy reunion after a period of sad separation.

Father A dream about your father reveals that you will be involved in a difficult situation which you will need wise advice in order to solve.

Fear To dream of fear shows that your future engagements will not be successful.

Laughter The happy laughter of children signifies joy and health.

Mother To hear your mother call out to you means that you are making a bad business decision.

Wedding If you attend a wedding in your dreams, this reveals that you are approaching a period of bitterness and delayed success.

Astrology

I n India, the most popular method of divination and means of influencing one's luck has for many years been astrology. Methods of astronomy and astrology were borrowed from the Chaldeans of Mesopotamia and later the Greeks. These include the twelve signs of the zodiac, the seven-day week, and the twenty-four hour day.

Astrology is a science based on the belief that our destinies are governed by the heavenly bodies (i.e. the planets, their moons, and the stars), acting singly as well as in groups called constellations. References to this science of horoscopy, or *hora-shastra*, are found in ancient Sanskrit texts. (The word "hora" originated in Greece and is the word for "hour".) Working from the position of the planets and stars at the time of your birth, an astrologer can chart your personal horoscope.

However educated or logical, almost every Indian believes in the power of astrology, consulting the stars before venturing on any new project. The horoscopes of the bride and groom are always compared when a marriage is being arranged; a lucky time is decided upon before entering a new home or conducting an auspicious ceremony. Certain times are considered universally auspicious, and these typically constitute the wedding season in India. These are the *uttarayana*, or period between the winter and summer solstices, and the Hindu month of Vaishakha, which falls between April and May. Hindu months do not follow a rigid pattern like the Gregorian calendar followed in the West; instead, they are based on lunar phases and the waxing and the waning of the moon. Thus each month has two sections, or *pakshas*. The half during which the moon waxes is the bright half, called *shukla paksha*, and the half in which it wanes is known as the dark half, or *krishna paksha*.

Astrologers consider many factors, including the place of birth, the season, the *paksh*, the birthdate, and the conjunction of the planets, the moon and the stars. When we talk of planets influencing a person, there is a minimum and a maximum period during which this can occur. The minimum period for an auspicious influence is called a *muhurta* and lasts forty-eight minutes. One of the commonest muhurtas is for marriage. When an auspicious time for a wedding is set, it is chosen so that there will be an abundance of love and luck. The maximum period of auspicious influence is one hundred and eight years, but such a lengthy period is extremely rare.

How does astrology work?

Astrology presents us with the possibilities, capabilities, and limitations that exist in each of us. How we develop these or overcome them depends on our own will. We are given clues, and it is for us to decide which path to follow. Astrology shows us the weak spots in our personality and the reason why we are not successful in certain endeavors. It also forewarns of certain unlucky periods when misfortune or calamity may strike. Through astrology, we can judge for ourselves the career to which we are best suited and the most fruitful times for making important decisions. Astrology is a predictive science, but no astrologer can determine how preordained events will influence an individual or how the individual will react to them. This depends on the person's own will, experience, and maturity.

The Zodiac

All planets exist within a belt that spans 360 degrees. This is divided into twelve houses, each measuring 30 degrees. The signs of the zodiac represent the constellations occupying each house. When a person is born or an event occurs, a degree in one of the twelve signs of the zodiac will be rising on the eastern horizon. More than any other, this ascendant sign influences one's life and personality. The Hindu zodiac consists of lunar signs plotted on rectangular chart (see below), whereas the Western system comprises solar signs arranged in a circle (see opposite). Because the sun is fixed, Western signs recur in a regular sequence (see page 18), but the position of Hindu signs varies each year, following the phases of the moon.

The Western and Hindu signs of the zodiac

Aquarius or Kumbha	300°–330°
Pisces or Meena	330°–360°
Aries or Mesha	0°–30°
Taurus or Vrishabha	30°–60°
Gemini or Mithuna	60°–90°
Cancer or Karkata	90°–120°
Leo or Simha	120°–150°
Virgo or Kanya	150°–180°
Libra or Tula	180°–210°
Scorpio or Vrishchik	210°–240°
Sagittarius or Dhanu	240°–270°
Capricorn or Makara	270°–300°

12. Meena	1. Mesha	2. Vrishabha	3. Mithuna
11. Kumbha			4. Karkata
10. Makara			5. Simha
9. Dhanu	8. Vrishchik	7. Tula	6. Kanya

A Horoscope Chart

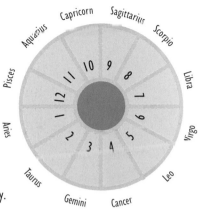

If you have had your chart drawn by an astrologer, you will see that it shows the position of the planets at the time of your birth. This unique constellation of the heavenly bodies will influence the course of your life and every aspect of your personality.

The first house signifies one's physical appearance. This is usually the house of Aries, ruled by Mars.

The second house shows one's financial position. It is ordinarily the house of Taurus, ruled by Venus.

The third house, which is usually Gemini, ruled by Mercury, signifies brothers, sisters, and mental outlook.

The fourth house, usually Cancer, governed by the moon, represents one's mother, father, childhood, and property.

The fifth house, usually Leo, governed by the sun, signifies love affairs, children, entertainment, and speculation.

The sixth house, the house of health, usually Virgo, ruled by Mercury, signifies care of the body, hygiene, grandparents, and servants.

The seventh house, usually Libra, ruled by Venus, signifies marriage, business, partnerships, and enemies.

The eighth house, usually Scorpio, ruled by Mars, tells us about death and inheritance.

The ninth house, usually Sagittarius, governed by Jupiter, signifies religion, philosophy, and travel.

The tenth house, usually Capricorn, ruled by Saturn, shows fame, ambition, power, position, and success in business.

The eleventh house, usually Aquarius, ruled by Uranus, concerns friendships and feelings of communal harmony.

The twelfth house, usually Pisces, ruled by Neptune, shows unseen difficulties, secret enemies, any impairment of the senses, seclusion, and subservience to others.

Characteristics of the heavenly bodies and signs of the zodiac

Those born to the same zodiacal sign share characteristics. However, there can be significant differences between two people born a few moments apart, due to slight changes in the degree of the ascendant and the position of the moon, which is why twins' personalities are often dissimilar.

Sun People born beneath the sign of Leo are wellbuilt with a broad forehead, curly hair and piercing eyes. Confident and masterful by nature, they are able to rise above the situation into which they were born.

Moon People born beneath the sign of Cancer are influenced by the moon. They are fair with a round face, bright eyes, and short arms and legs. They are mild and well intentioned but also timid and thoughtless. The moon is the most sensitive of the celestial bodies and is influenced by all the other planets. Hence, these people can vary greatly in temperament.

Mercury People born beneath the signs of Gemini and Virgo are influenced by Mercury. They are tall with a straight nose, narrow face, an active and witty mind, an excellent memory, and an aptitude for public speaking. However, this planet takes on the vibrations of other planets, and if Mercury is not present in conjunction with beneficial planets, an individual will be stingy, conceited, and a liar.

Venus Librans and Taurians are born when Venus is in the ascendant. These people are beautiful with sparkling eyes and a smooth face. They may also have a sweet voice and dimples. Venus encourages them to follow the line of least resistance, and they are generally unwilling to make great sacrifices in

order to achieve great things. Those influenced
by Venus win many friends and have favors
showered upon them. For them, love is
paramount and early marriage is not uncommon,
but the attraction is largely physical, and once the
novelty has worn off, Venus encourages them to stray.

Mars People born beneath the signs of Aries and Scorpio are
influenced by Mars. They are strong and muscular with sharp
eyes. Many also have a scar on the head or face. A strong Mars ascendancy
makes people fearless, forthright, and generous, but an ill-aspected Mars
makes them angry, cruel, quarrelsome, and wicked. Of course, it is up to the
individual to utilize the force of this planet in a constructive way.

Jupiter Sagittarians are influenced by Jupiter. People with a strong Jupiter
ascendancy are physically robust, ruddy, and tall, with a character that is
authoritative, jovial, and spiritually inclined. However, people born beneath
a weak Jupiter are careless, conceited, and prone to religious fanaticism.
Jupiter is the symbol of wisdom. It is also a very "lucky" planet, assuring
success in all endeavors, but its effects will be influenced by other planets
in its vicinity.

Saturn Bearing on the sign of Capricorn, Saturn is identified with obstacles
and isolation. The effect of a strong Saturn is most evident in the first
thirty years of a person's life and then again after the sixtieth year. If you
have a strong Saturn ascendancy, you must be prepared to endure and
overcome several obstacles in your life, but this energetic planet also
provides the stamina needed to overcome adversity. Perseverance is of
utmost importance, as projects abandoned half-way through will lead to
nothing but depression and bitterness. Unselfish service is the surest
means to counteracting a strong Saturn.

Uranus Because this planet was discovered around 200 years ago it is not
recorded in ancient Indian texts. Modern astrology suggests that people
influenced by Uranus, Aquarians in particular, are intuitive and
compassionate. People with a strong Uranus ascendancy have greatly
fluctuating fortunes, both in the amount of wealth they possess and in the
careers they pursue. They are also philosophical and prophetic. An extremely
strong Uranus can mar relationships and encourage extreme self-
centeredness, while a weak Uranus makes people brusque and headstrong.

Neptune Influencing those born beneath Pisces, this mystical planet makes
people forthright. Guided by their dreams, clairvoyance, and intuition, they
are also able to view situations in their entirety and foresee what lies
around the corner. A weak Neptune makes people fickle and impractical.
They also worry a great deal and often fall ill as a result.

How a horoscope is cast

Astrology is a science that requires years of deep study in order to be fully comprehended. Many intricate details can dramatically alter the messages contained in a horoscope, and learning to decipher these takes commitment to learning and a lifetime of experience.

Before you can cast a horoscope you will need the following essential information:

The exact time of birth; even a minute here or there could dramatically alter the horoscope.

The year, date, and latitude and longitude of the place of birth.

Intricate calculations are then made using the local time to reveal the exact time of birth, called the "sidereal time of birth." Further calculations determine the position of the sun, the moon and the various planets, using charts that provide guidelines as to the local times, latitudes, and longitudes. This is an exercise that requires considerable skill, as each planet's position at the time of birth relative to birthplace has to be determined. The horoscope is then cast, providing guidelines for a person's entire life.

Palmistry

The Sanskrit word for hand, *hasta*, suggests that it is a tool for the acquisition of possessions. In every Indian language, there are many definitions of hand, from "that which grips" and "having five branches" to "that which bestows tranquillity" and "that through which we experience." The ancients believed that the hand was a powerful medium, a potent vehicle of divine energy. Through the hand, a person could heal, make donations, and give strength or even life, but it could also injure, seize, or kill. Even an imprint of the hand was considered a fragment of divinity, which was capable of providing protection. It is not uncommon to see rural dwellings in India marked with colorful imprints of the owners' hands, as people believe these marks ensure that their homes are guarded during their absence.

History of palmistry

The great seer and occult researcher Cheiro (1866–1936) wrote:

To consider the origin of this science [palmistry], we must take our thoughts back to the earliest days of the world's history, and furthermore to the consideration of a people who are the oldest of all ... those children of the East, the Hindus, a people whose philosophy and wisdom are every day being more and more revived.

... in the northwest province of India, palmistry was practiced and followed by the Joshi caste from time immemorial to the present day. ... A book I was allowed to use during my sojourn in India was one of the greatest treasures of the Brahmins who possessed and understood it. This strange book was made of human skin, was of enormous size, and contained hundreds of well-drawn illustrations with records of how, when, and where this or that mark was proved correct. One of its strangest features was that it was written in some red liquid which age had failed to spoil or fade.

Palmistry, or the study of the hand with its lines, mounts, and hollows, originated in India but was later practiced by the Chinese, Persians, Greeks, and Egyptians. In Greece, it came to be called cheiromancy, from the Greek *cheir*, for "hand," and was practiced as far back as 423 B.C.

The lines on your hand

Each person possesses a unique pair of hands. According to palmists, the left hand describes your constitution, and the right hand reveals what you will acquire and make of yourself. It is a myth that lines on the hand are caused simply by hard, physical work. If this were so, laborers would have a maze of lines and a king would have none. We also see that newborn babies with not a scrap of work to their name already have lines on their hands. Furthermore, there are countless lines on the palm that do not correspond to movement of the hand. The lines on our palms are believed to be caused by our emotions such as anger or affection, being expressed by our movements. These movements are harsh or graceful, depending on the emotion they express, and therefore produce large or small lines on the palm. Creases and lines are therefore a direct indication of emotions expressed through movement.

Shapes of hands

Palmists look at a hand in its entirety, from the lines on the palm to even the fine hair on the back of the hand. There are seven shapes of hand, and these describe different personality types:

The elementary hand This looks coarse and clumsy and has few lines. These people are generally indifferent to beauty or aesthetics. They are temperamental but never ambitious.

The square hand Also called the useful hand, this denotes a reliable personality, which excels at the practical side of things. Such people identify what needs to be done and set about doing it with methodical precision. In the process, they can appear insensitive and inflexible.

The spatulate hand This is often known as the nervous or active hand. This hand is characterized firstly by the tips of the fingers, which resemble spatulas, and secondly by the fact that the hand itself is broader at the wrist or at the base of the fingers than at the fingertips. This hand belongs to a person who is full of enthusiasm and excitement but finds perseverance nearly impossible, and whose work follows an irregular

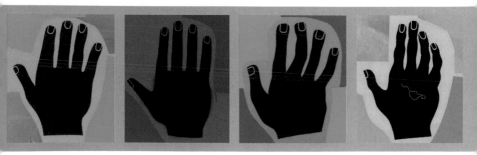

pattern. However, these people undertake tasks that interest them with great zeal and spirit, and they succeed in creating new ways of thinking. Many discoverers and voyagers have spatulate hands.

The philosophic or knotty hand   This is usually long and angular and has bony fingers, prominent joints, and long nails. Knotty joints signify a love for the philosophical, while smooth fingers denote a materialistic nature. Hence, these people are more concerned with the philosophy of life than with the material means to sustain it. Money is not important to them. They love mystical subjects and add a sense of mystery to everything they touch. They are silent, thinking types who can be quite egotistical.

The conical or artistic hand   This is a medium-sized palm which tapers toward the area below the fingers. The fingers are slightly pointed at the tips. These people are impulsive and act on instinct. If the hand is soft, it indicates a love of luxury, a good measure of impatience, and a tendency to grow bored before a task is complete. People with a conical hand are easily influenced and parted from their money. Although the conical hand is also called the artistic hand, these people may not be intrinsically artistic. They are simply more affected by aspects of their environment, including color, music, speech, tears, sorrow, or joy. If the hand is hard, the person will have a firm will and sparkling wit. This is the hand of a true performer who relies on emotion to win people over.

The psychic or idealistic hand   This is the loveliest but the most jinxed of all the hand shapes. It is long, narrow, and fragile in appearance with slender, pointed fingers and perfect, oval nails. These people are idealistic, flippant, and impractical. They are attracted to mysticism and the occult but hate to be deceived. They are quick to tune in to other people's feelings and therefore make good clairvoyants and mediums.

The mixed hand   This hand reveals a potpourri of characteristics. These people are adept at transforming a situation and adjusting to change and new circumstances. They are all-round achievers and will have several interests at one time. They make friends easily and sail through life with no worries about the future.

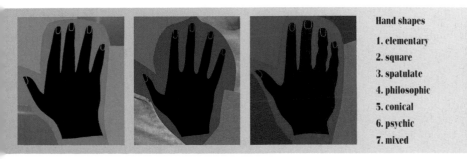

Hand shapes
1. elementary
2. square
3. spatulate
4. philosophic
5. conical
6. psychic
7. mixed

The lines on the hand

Illustrated opposite, there are seven main lines on the palm:

The line of life signifies health and death.

The line of the head signifies intellectual capacity.

The line of the heart signifies love.

The girdle of Venus signifies moodiness and emotional inflexibility.

The line of health signifies well-being. Absence of this line signifies excellent health.

The line of the Sun signifies success. A prominent line indicates fame and power.

The line of fate reveals worldly success or failure.

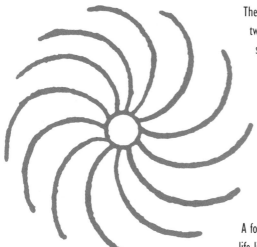

The hand is divided horizontally into two parts: the top part represents the spiritual self, whereas the bottom half signifies the material self. The lines of the hand should be clear and continuous, without breaks or irregularities. Certain features of each line reveal aspects of your personality:

A fork at the end of a line (except the life line) gives greater power to that line.

A tassel at the end of a line reveals a weakness around the particular characteristic that line represents.

Branches out of a line accentuate the power of that line, although descending branches indicate weakness.

A chain of islands, or loops, along any prominent line denotes a weak physique or intellect.

A network of lines spreading over the palm indicates a troubled nature, excessive worry, and restlessness.

A break in a line denotes failure.

GIRDLE OF VENUS

HEAD

HEART

MARRIAGE

MARS

LIFE

FATE

SUN

HEALTH

THE BRACELETS

Mounts of the hand

The raised portions of a palm, illustrated on page 60, reveal the temperament of its owner. The names given to the mounts are the same as those of the seven main planets governing the destiny of Earth. Each also represents a cluster of personality traits:

Mount of Venus	love, sensuality, passion
Mount of Mars	vitality, courage, spirit of war
Mount of Mercury	mentality, science, commerce
Mount of Moon	creativity, romance, changeability
Mount of Sun	success, brilliance, acceptance in the world
Mount of Jupiter	power, ambition, leadership
Mount of Saturn	melancholy, seriousness, leadership

The mount of Venus lies under the base of the thumb. A well-formed mount indicates a desire for love and companionship, an appreciation of the arts and of beauty and the desire to make others happy. When very prominent, it indicates that the individual is very attractive to the opposite sex.

The mount of Mars has two positions on the hand: the first lies roughly in the middle of the outer edge of the palm in line with the little finger, and the second one lies directly opposite, between the thumb and the forefinger. When the first mount of Mars is prominent, the individual is headstrong and does not heed the advice of others. He or she also hates to be criticized and needs to be handled with kindness, love, and patience. Such a person is good-natured and expansive but fitful and impulsive in their actions. If the second mount of Mars is prominent, however, the individual is the opposite of the one described above, with a surfeit of moral courage rather than physical prowess.

The mount of Mercury lies at the base of the little finger. A good mount will signify an agile mind, capable of grasping the intricacies of thought and wisdom, but a weak one will denote nervousness, unscrupulous morals in business, and a lack of concentration.

The mount of the Moon is at the base of the palm under the first mount of Mars. People with a prominent mount are highly romantic but can be idealistic in their desires. They lack the passion of Venus. These people succeed when a lively imagination is required.

The mount of the Sun lies at the base of the ring finger. A well-developed mount indicates fame and a positive public image. These people are generous and have very good taste. They are positive in their outlook and appear dashing and confident to others.

The mount of Jupiter lies at the base of the index finger. When prominent, it implies a dominating personality and the wish to lead others. However, these people sometimes take things to an extreme in their zeal to reach their goal.

The mount of Saturn lies at the base of the middle finger. A developed mount points to a love of solitude and serious pursuits, a fatalistic view of life and a steady, silent determination to pursue one's own way of life. Such people are often perceived as gloomy or serious. In contrast, an under-developed mount indicates a frivolous personality.

The fingers

A beautifully proportioned hand always draws the attention of a viewer. Long fingers are considered beautiful. They signify attention to detail and a love of aesthetics and constancy.

Short-fingered people are quick and impulsive and jump to conclusions very easily. Clumsy and short fingers belong to someone who is cruel and selfish. When the fingers are stiff and curve inward, the person is extremely cautious and can be a coward. Supple fingers that can bend backward are seen on a person who is clever and a sparkling conversationalist, but who is also inordinately curious. Crooked fingers denote an evil heart that feeds a wicked mind.

The nails

In palmistry, nails have their own story to tell. They are an accurate guide to the health of an individual, including any chronic illnesses and hereditary traits. There are four nail types:

Long nails	impressionable, calm, artistic
Short nails	critical, analytical, good sense of humor
Broad nails	tendency to worry, inquisitive, interfering
Narrow nails	weak-minded, selfish, secretive

Health

May I nourish myself with juices of fruits obtained from this earth.
May I nourish myself with medicinal plants.
Yajur-Veda (c. 700–300 B.C.)

I grew up with the proverb that health is wealth. My family believed in diligent hard work, but never at the cost of one's health. My grandmother would say, "If money is lost, little is lost, if time is lost, a lot is lost, but if health is lost, everything is lost." If you do not have good health, all the money and time in the world are of no use to you. On the other hand, a fit and balanced body and mind can help you work miracles with your destiny.

India is acknowledged internationally as the treasury of Ayurvedic wisdom, in which natural herbs, seeds, fruits, flowers, barks, and leaves are used to heal and fortify the body. Many thousands of years ago, certain plants were considered sacred, and their use and applications evolved into a medical science called Ayurveda. This system of gentle, natural medicine is fast gaining popularity the world over. Its remedies are safe and address the root of the problem rather than treating its symptoms, as is the case with modern medicine. It is an all-encompassing science which offers marvelous cures for contemporary problems, such as stress-induced muscular aches and high blood cholesterol.

Ayurveda is best understood as a complete way of life, dedicated to the enhancement of human life. It was developed many centuries ago in the Himalayan mountains, where valleys of flowers and herbs blossomed in the pristine air. This science of life (*ayur* meaning "life" and *veda* meaning "knowledge") touched upon all aspects of well-being (physical, mental, and spiritual), and its main objective, as with modern medicine, was to prolong life without disease. In India, people follow many healing traditions, ranging from Ayurveda and allopathy to homeopathy and acupressure. Natural healing comes in many forms, including massage, a controlled diet, approved drugs, exercise, special baths, and steam inhalation.

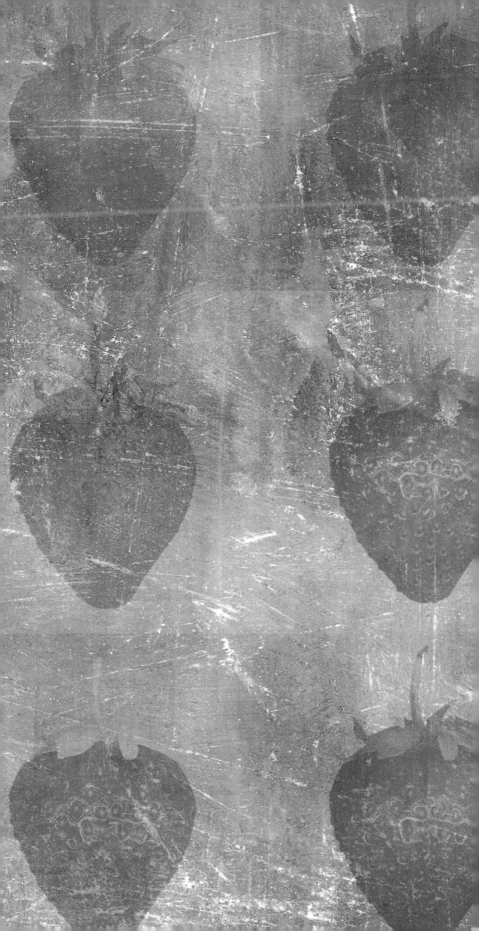

Black mustard seeds held over a beleaguered person and burned in a pan are said to guard against ill luck.

While Indians follow varied medicinal traditions, they also seek "health luck" to bolster healing and speed recovery. Often, people with chronic disorders wear lucky talismans in order to make their situation tolerable. As I have said before, however, belief is all. If you trust your luck tool to work for you, it will. That is why, despite having modernization at my fingertips and a mind that can be maddeningly cynical, I still follow a quaint tradition passed down by generations of Indian women. My grandmother and mother followed it, and I find myself following it as faithfully as they did. Each night, I wave a handful of black mustard seeds over my children's heads at bedtime to remove negativity and guard against accident and ill health. My faith has often seen a sick child become visibly better before my eyes.

IMPORTANT All the luck remedies listed here MUST be used in conjunction with professional medical advice. None of these tools offer a guaranteed cure.

Gems & health

Throughout history gems have been used for luck and healing. In ancient India, gems were worn as amulets or even crushed and drunk to counteract sickness or malaise. The ruby was said to be an antidote to poison, and diamonds were said to usher in an easy childbirth. Early Egyptians wore a turquoise to safeguard their spiritual self. Today, people still wear gems for health luck, and this is based largely on the color of the stone, each color bearing different health luck properties:

red or pink gems (ruby, garnet, rose quartz) These are usually associated with blood, heat, and energy. In gem healing, the ruby is best used for treating heart disease and poor circulation. It also treats anemia and eye diseases. Rose quartz is gentle and encourages inner peace, generosity, and calmness.

orange gems (amber, coral) These are generally associated with the digestive system and immunity. Coral is considered to be a universal healer. It is used to guard against accidents, arthritis, constipation, gout, hysteria, paralysis, miscarriage, and sexual diseases. Even little babies are given a tiny coral to wear around their wrist to ward off ills and pains.

yellow gems (topaz, yellow sapphire, citrine, tiger's eye) Yellow gems govern the nerves and the nervous system. Topaz is used for asthma, laryngitis, insomnia, bites, infections, burns, shock, childhood diseases, and nervous exhaustion. Tiger's eye, with its high iron content, is used for indigestion, skin and blood problems, and migraine headaches.

green gems (emerald, jade, tourmaline) These gems are used for general healing and for stress. Emerald treats typhoid, leucoderma, insomnia, high blood pressure, and cancer.

Jade is considered pure, lucky, and an effective treatment for kidney and bladder trouble. It also helps to develop a clear-thinking mind, free from confusion and worry.

blue gems (sapphire, turquoise, lapis lazuli) Blue gems enhance the mental faculties and creativity. Sapphire treats cancer, asthma, insomnia, hypertension, and nervousness. Aquamarine is used for problems of the mouth, throat, and neck. It also treats nerve and glandular pains.

purple gems (amethyst) Purple gems inspire spirituality and soothe deep-rooted pains. Amethyst treats insomnia, headaches, and all kinds of emotional and physical pain.

white gems (diamond, pearl, opal, white coral, moonstone) Diamond treats impotence, paralysis, eye problems, and epilepsy. Pearl is used for asthma, menstrual problems, piles, and problems of digestion. In India, brides wear pearls to ensure a happy married life and for protection from widowhood.

black gems (jet, obsidian, smoky quartz, black coral) Black gems are known to absorb negative energy and protect the wearer from evil vibrations. This is especially significant in India, where people wear black gems to protect themselves from the envy or ill will of others.

Color & health

We can feel lucky only if we are healthy. Color healing has long been a part of the ancient Indian medical repertoire. It is now supplemented by color acupuncture and color vibrations, to treat pain and help patients recover faster.

Color in food

We all know that our appetite and appreciation of food depends largely upon its appearance and beauty. Natural colors in food appeal to us, whereas bright, synthetic colors repel. The traditional Indian diet contains a palette of colors—saffrons, golds, greens, crimsons, and browns—which are visually appealing and help to stimulate health and energy. Indians also tend to cook foods in ways that preserve their color and nutritional value.

Foods contain the energy of cosmic rays that correspond to their natural color. If you constantly eat foods of a particular color, but do not notice their color as much as their taste, this can indicate something wrong with your health.

How food colors influence our health

Colors	Action	Foods	Organs affected	Results
red foods	warming, stimulating	berries, red apples, red kidney beans, iron-rich vegetables, meat, tomatoes, foods of animal origin, radishes	kidney, bladder, muscular system	excessive amounts of red foods cause anger, irritablity, and hyperactivity
orange foods	tonic, appetite-building, anti-depressant	mangoes, carrots, peaches, egg yolk, pumpkin, papaya, orange peppers	legs, stomach, circulatory system	orange helps protect against air pollution and the sun's harmful ultraviolet rays
yellow foods	cleansing, laxative, harmonizing	yellow lentils, beans, and grains, bananas, pineapple, corn, lemons	stomach, liver, nervous system	yellow calms the mind and promotes happiness and well-being
green foods	calming, relaxing	green grapes, okra, coriander, peas, green beans, whole mung beans, cucumber, milk and its products	ears, arms, digestive system, heart	milk imparts the green energy of the grass from which it originates
blue foods	antiseptic, soporific, soothing	raisins, blueberries, blackberries, blue plums, prunes, mushrooms	mouth, throat, respiratory system	blue induces calm and restful sleep, without tension or nightmares
purple foods	anti-bacterial, deeply soothing, induce creativity	eggplants, beets, and purple onions, cabbage, and grapes	scalp, hair, pituitary gland	purple has the soothing effect of blue and the energizing effect of red; thus is nutritious but not overly stimulating

Color and your chakras

Although there are said to be more than eighty-eight thousand chakras (yogic centers of psychic energy) in the body, seven of these are especially significant. Each of these absorbs a particular color vibration through light and disperses it throughout the body. It is well known in Ayurveda that when any of these chakras is unhealthy, due to blocked energies, a person will feel unwell. Each chakra is associated with the health of certain parts of the body, and the color associated with that chakra will help heal them. The seven abstract chakras are associated with the following:

muladhara chakra at the base of the spine, is associated with red energy, the kidneys, and the arteries.

swadhishthana chakra in the small of the back, absorbs orange energy and affects the reproductive organs. This chakra is connected with the excitement of sexual feelings.

manipura chakra in the lumbar region absorbs yellow vibrations and affects sleep and thirst. This chakra, when healthy, can help relieve pain.

anahata chakra situated in the heart, absorbs green energy and is associated with the heart and the circulation. It also governs hope, anxiety, doubt, and remorse, so keeping it healthy is essential.

vishuddha chakra in the throat, absorbs blue energy and governs the throat, especially the larynx, which is responsible for speech.

ajna chakra situated between the eyebrows, is linked to purple and governs the realm of concentration and consciousness. It also affects the pituitary gland and the senses of smell, sight, and taste.

sahasrara chakra lies about four finger-breadths above the crown of the head and therefore lies outside the body. It is what some doctrines call a halo, and it absorbs magenta rays. This chakra influences the spiritual health and is called the vessel of immortality, which contains the elusive nectar of life. Many yoga practitioners attempt to conquer this chakra in order to attain immortality.

How to keep the chakras healthy

Specific yoga exercises keep the chakras healthy and responsive to color influences. When working on a specific chakra, visualize the color associated with it, so that you give your health luck the best chance. Do each exercise until you feel revitalized:

muladhara chakra (red) Open your palm and make gentle circular movements over the base of your spine until you feel relaxed and energized.

swadhishthana chakra (orange) Using your palm, gently massage the lower back and the lower portion of your stomach.

manipura chakra (yellow) Gently massage your stomach with your open palm until you feel a complete sense of well-being.

anahata chakra (green) Lightly tap your thymus gland (at the top of the chest) with you left hand, and then make soft circles over the chest.

vishuddha chakra (blue) With the fingertips, gently drum on either side of the neck, on each shoulder, and down the arms, then back up again to the neck.

ajna chakra (purple) With the middle and ring finger of the right hand, press the area between the eyebrows, where the third eye is located. One of the reasons why Hindus wear a *bindi*, or a dot, on the forehead is to highlight this chakra, which is the center of consciousness.

sahasrara chakra (magenta) Make tiny circles just above the crown of your head with your open palm until you feel focused and strong.

Symbols & health

Peole in India believe that symbols are carriers of good luck. Although auspicious symbols are still used to invite luck into one's life in a general way, ancient sages gave ritualistic meaning to certain symbols, and therefore some remain particularly important for health luck.

the swastika The ancient Aryan people who settled in India and Iran revered the sun as a source of energy and life. They created a radiant, golden-bodied deity called Surya, or the sun god, who brings light and power on his mythical chariot. A unique graphical symbol was conceived to represent the sun's eternal energy and benevolence. This was the swastika, a four-armed, squarish wheel seemingly poised to rotate in a clockwise direction, a shape that was held to capture the good luck of the four cardinal directions. In twentieth-century Europe the swastika was reversed and became a symbol of fear and hatred, but in India it is still considered one of the most sacred and powerful symbols.

Hindus paint the swastika on walls, wear it as jewelry, and draw it on furniture as an everlasting sign of luck. Being a symbol of the sun, it is often crafted in pure gold and worn as a locket to ward against danger and disease. The word "swastika" means well-being, and its abbreviated form (*swasti*) is commonly used in ceremonial chants. A good-luck posture, or *asana*, in yoga represents the swastika. Called *swastikasana*, it involves sitting with one's arms and legs crossed.

the third eye Another potent symbol used to inspire health luck is the third eye. Legends talk of gods opening the third eye to send forth flashes of lightning and destroy evil forces. In Indian art, Hindu gods and goddesses, in particular Shiva the Destroyer and Durga the Remover of Evil, are depicted with an open, alert eye in the center of their forehead. Yoga philosophy also stipulates that every human being possesses an unseen third eye, which is the seat of immense occult power.

An oil lamp is symbolic of prosperity. When lit, it creates an ambiance that is festive and ethereal.

The overlapping associations of the third eye confuse many people, but this symbol is still considered a powerful means of ensuring spiritual health and well-being. It represents the ability of the human mind to see beyond the material world to the inner core of life, which is the source of divine energy. The concept of the third eye rests on the belief that people who think independently and commune with their inner selves will find peace, truth, and spiritual health.

Metals & health

I ndia's ancient traditions promote the healing power of lucky metals. Gold is considered fortunate, but silver in particular is thought to inspire health luck. In ancient times, people believed that the cooling powers of silver could calm fevers, soothe the brain, and attract the healing forces of the moon.

Of all the metals, however, copper is that most closely associated with health. The early Indians believed that it possessed magical healing properties, and while storytellers described gold as a fragment of the sun, the astrologers linked the sun to copper. Traditional Indian medicines still rely on the fiery properties of this metal in order to combat high blood pressure. Many people will wear a copper bracelet or drink water stored overnight in a copper container. One of Ayurveda's most potent health tonics contains *tamra bhasma*, a copper powder. The healing power of copper can be supplemented by wearing a bracelet of *panch-dhatu*, the five auspicious metals—namely gold, silver, copper, bronze, and iron. This bracelet helps to maintain good overall health and vigor.

Hindu astrology pairs metals with planets. Just as copper is identified with the Sun, gold is paired with Mars and iron with Saturn, while silver is associated with the Moon and Jupiter. Each of us can obtain health luck from a specific metal, named in our personal horoscope, which contains the properties of its reigning planet and targets specific problems:

Metals and their planets

Metal	Planet	Body part governed	Conditions Relieved
Copper	Sun	back, heart, arteries, eyes, and retentive faculties	high blood pressure, palpitation, weak eyesight
Gold	Mars	head, face, stomach, kidneys, knees, bladder, groin, circulation, reproduction system	inflammation of wounds and burns, tumors, abcesses, headaches, toothache, diabetes, jaundice, shingles, carbuncles, fevers
Silver	Jupiter	liver, lungs, blood, veins	liver disease
Silver	Moon	brain, stomach, bowels, bladder, breasts, lymph glands	rheumatism, vertigo, colic, palsy, smallpox, apoplexy, lunacy
Iron	Saturn	nose, respiratory system, lungs, ears, throat	colds, catarrh, atrophy, fistula, leprosy, deafness, epilepsy, tonsillitis, diphtheria, swollen throat

Foods

Astrology and traditional medicine both maintain that the planets are somehow present in certain foods, and that by consuming these foods we can enhance our health luck. This lore can be reproduced within the Western zodiac:

Aquarius	Saturn	black sesame seeds
Pisces	Jupiter	chickpeas
Aries	Mars	yellow lentils
Taurus	Venus	black-eyed peas
Gemini	Mercury	mung beans
Cancer	Moon	rice
Leo	Sun	wheat
Virgo	Mercury	mung beans
Libra	Venus	black-eyed peas
Scorpio	Mars	yellow lentils
Sagittarius	Jupiter	chickpeas
Capricorn	Saturn	black sesame seeds

These healing foods are used in a variety of nutritious Indian recipes. Here are some for you to try:

Yellow Lentil Shorba Serves 4

This delicious soup makes a sustaining lunch served with nan bread.

ingredients

¾ cup (170g) yellow lentils
3½ cups (750ml) water
1 tablespoon sunflower oil
1 teaspoon black mustard seeds
1 teaspoon cumin seeds
1 large pinch asafetida powder
1 teaspoon tamarind paste, soaked and blended with
    1 tablepoon (15ml) water
1 large pinch sugar
1 teaspoon turmeric powder
1 teaspoon chili powder
1 teaspoon ground coriander
Salt to taste
2 tablespoons cilantro leaves, to garnish

1. Boil the lentils in the water for 15 minutes until soft and pulpy.

2. Heat the oil in a heavy pan. Add the mustard seeds. When they crackle, drop in the cumin and asafetida, then the tamarind paste.

3. Stir and allow to boil, adding a little extra water to prevent it from drying out, if necessary. Add the next five ingredients, and simmer for a minute or so.

4. Add the cooked lentils. Stir well, check the seasoning, and serve hot, garnished with fresh cilantro leaves.

Black-eyed Pea Curry Serves 4

Full of nourishment, black-eyed peas make a filling and flavorful curry.

ingredients

1 cup (230g) dried black-eyed
    peas
5 tablespoons sunflower oil
generous ½ cup (70g) finely
    chopped onions
generous ½ cup (70g) finely
    chopped tomatoes
1 teaspoon ginger paste
1 teaspoon garlic paste
1 teaspoon turmeric

I teaspoon chili powder
I teaspoon coriander powder
I teaspoon garam masala
Salt to taste
Cilantro leaves, freshly chopped, to garnish.

1. Soak the beans overnight, then drain and rinse them.

2. Heat two tablespoons of the oil. When hot, add the onions and fry gently until translucent. Add the ginger, garlic paste, and tomatoes. Fry well over a low heat until it forms a thick paste.

3. Mash the paste coarsely, then add the soaked peas. Sprinkle in the turmeric, chili powder, ground coriander, garam masala, and salt. Stir thoroughly. Add 4½ cups (1 liter) of water and bring to the boil.

4. Lower the heat and simmer, adding more water as necessary, until the peas are tender. You should have a thick, fragrant curry. Garnish with chopped cilantro, and serve hot with nan or other bread.

Mung Beans on Toast Serves 4

Enjoy this as a healthful
breakfast which provides
the energy you need for
a busy working day.

ingredients

¾ cup (170g) dried mung beans
Salt to taste
4 slices brown bread
Butter to taste
1¼ cup (300ml) natural yogurt
Fruit, such as papaya, melon, or banana, sliced, to serve

1. Soak the beans overnight. In the morning, drain and rinse the beans, then wrap them in a soft, porous cloth, and knot the ends of the cloth together. Hang up the bundle, away from moisture. Depending on the weather, the beans will soon begin to sprout. Allow the sprouts to grow to ¼ inch (5mm) long.

2. Put the beans in a vegetable steamer or a colander over a pan of boiling water. Cook the beans until they are just tender and still crunchy. Remove and add salt.

3. Toast and butter the bread. Top with the mung beans.

4. Serve each slice hot with a bowl of yogurt on the side as an accompaniment and with a slice of your favorite fruit. Try papaya, melon, or banana.

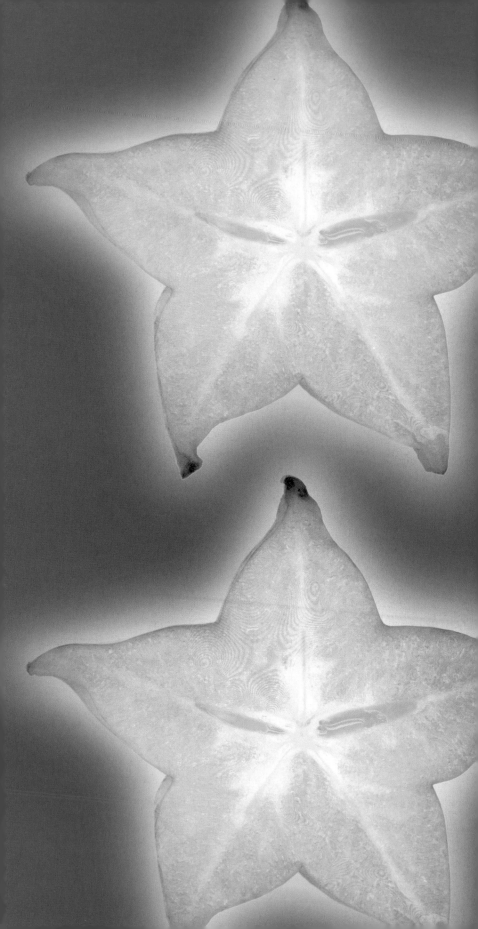

Chickpeas in Coconut Milk Serves 4

Coconut milk adds a rich flavor to these spicy chickpeas.

ingredients

>2 tablespoons sunflower oil
>1 teaspoon cumin seeds
>1 teaspoon ground turmeric
>1 teaspoon chili powder
>1 teaspoon ground coriander
>Salt to taste
>1¼ cup (300 ml) coconut milk
>1 x size 300 (13oz [385g]) can of chickpeas
>2 tablespoons cilantro leaves, freshly chopped, to garnish

1. Heat the oil in a heavy pan and add the cumin seeds. Stir and add the turmeric, chili powder, ground coriander, and salt.

2. Pour in the coconut milk, and simmer over low heat until the milk starts to thicken.

3. Drain the chickpeas, add to the pan, and heat through.

4. Garnish with chopped cilantro leaves, and serve hot with plain boiled rice and a fresh salad.

Sesame Seed Chutney Serves 4

This can be eaten with nans and a fresh green salad.

ingredients

>2 tablespoons (30ml) sunflower oil
>4 tablespoons (60ml) black sesame seeds
>4 tablespoons (60ml) white sesame seeds
>½ cup (100g) unsalted peanuts
>2 garlic cloves, finely chopped
>½ cup (40g) shredded coconut
>Salt to taste
>1 tablespoon (15ml) tamarind paste

1. Heat the oil in a pan and gently fry all the ingredients, except the salt and tamarind, until brown.

2. Mix in the salt and tamarind, and grind to a coarse powder in a blender.

3. Store in an airtight jar, and use within three weeks.

✳ Vastu shastra & health

We can improve our health by applying the principles of Vastu Shastra to our daily lives. This is primarily a science of construction, in which homes, offices, and other buildings are built in ways that improve their owners' fortunes. In essence, Vastu Shastra seeks optimum contact between the five elements—earth, water, fire, air, and space—and the natural energies of the planets, in order to create balance and harmony within a dwelling. When homes are built in keeping with the principles of Vastu Shastra, one's luck in health, wealth, and relationships will be increased.

As we all know, it is crucial that there be ample amounts of light and air in any home to ensure a healthy environment for its inhabitants. According to Vastu Shastra, windows should be placed to promote cross-ventilation and allow the maximum amount of light to enter. Furthermore, rooms that face favorable directions are beneficial to health, while illness may occur in those that do not.

Vastu Shastra and direction of rooms

Room	Good direction	Bad direction	Ill effects
living room	northeast, east	south	intermittent ill health
main bedroom	southwest, south	northeast	emotional upsets constant ills
children's bedrooom	west	east	illness in children, loss of a child
dining room	southeast, west	northeast	expenses, anxiety
kitchen	southeast, north	east	women suffer from health problems and are unhappy, despite their material comfort
bathroom	east	west	inhabitants suffer from lack of energy, and ill health

Vastu Shastra identifies each of the eight directions with a planetary influence. Understanding these affinities can also improve one's health luck.

north The governing planet here is Mercury. In the home it is the area where money and valuable possessions should be stored safely. However, if food is stored here, the lady of the house and the children will be unhealthy.

northwest Here the presiding planet is Ketu. (Neptune and Uranus do not feature in Indian astrology, as they are later discoveries. Rahu and Ketu, points where the moon in its orbit intersects the cosmic equator, are recognized instead. Although not planets, they are counted as such because of their effects on mankind.) Never store old or broken objects in this area, as this causes poor health for all inhabitants; their complaints would include aching joints and headaches.

east This is governed by the Sun, as it is where the sun rises. Allow for as many east-facing doors and windows as possible, so that morning sunlight will flood the home, nourishing and energizing its occupants. The bathroom is ideally located in the east, so that bathers enjoy the Sun's cleansing rays. If the kitchen is east-facing, however, the woman of the house will suffer with bilious complaints, nervousness, and gynecological problems; the kitchen is governed by Venus, who has an unfavorable relationship with the Sun. Also, check for cracked doors and windows, which place inhabitants in danger of death.

southeast Venus rules over this direction. The kitchen is best located here. However, if stale food or great quantities of water are stored in the kitchen, the women of the house will suffer from ill health. It is important, therefore, that all food stored here be fresh and that leftovers be eaten quickly or disposed of.

south The south is governed by Mars, and the bedroom is ideally located here. The bed should be positioned so that one's head points toward the south. This is because the head acts as a magnet which will repel the north pole if placed facing north, resulting in headaches and tension. One must also be careful not to store any food in the bedroom, as this results in the man of the house feeling weak and lazy; all foods are governed by the Moon, who is unfriendly to Mars.

southwest The governing planet here is Rahu, the ascending node of the moon. This is the best location for a storeroom. If there is a bedroom here, the governing planets will clash, giving the woman of the house rheumatic ailments or mobility problems. If a dining room is situated here, the inhabitants will suffer from poor digestion or eye complaints. If the main door faces southwest, the owner of the house will have recurring ill health.

west This direction is ruled by Saturn. The dining room is best located in the west-facing portion of the house. If the inhabitants eat together in this part of the house, great health and luck will follow.

northwest This is the direction of the Moon and is ideal for the storage of pulses, grains, and dry ingredients. However, if the kitchen is situated here, medical problems for the women of the house will result.

Numbers & health

Numerology consists of a vast body of knowledge and touches upon many topics related to luck. For example, it describes which fruits, herbs, and plants suit individuals of a particular birth number. Numerology also discusses explicitly which diseases affect people of the same birth number. Your birth number is calculated by adding together the digits contained in your birth date (for example, people born on the twenty-seventh day of any month have a birth number of nine).

number one These people tend to suffer from heart problems, such as palpitation, poor circulation, or high blood pressure. They may also have eye problems, such as astigmatism, and should take the precaution of having regular eye tests. The best herbs and fruits for number one people are camomile, saffron, cloves, nutmeg, sorrel, borage, lavender, bay leaves, oranges, lemons, dates, thyme, ginger, and barley. They should also eat honey regularly. Number one people will find that the most significant changes in their health, for better or worse, will be in their nineteenth, twenty-eighth, thirty-seventh, and fifty-fifth years. They need to guard their health, and avoid overwork in the months of January, October, and December.

number two These people are most likely to be afflicted by problems of the stomach and digestive system. The foods best suited to them are lettuce, cabbage, melon, endive, linseed, cucumber, and turnips. The years that will show a marked change in their health will be their twentieth, twenty-fifth, twenty-ninth, forty-third, forty-seventh, fifty-second, and sixty-fifth years. Each year, they must pay close attention to their health during the months of January, February, and July.

number three They are inclined to strain their nervous systems through overwork and the relentless pursuit of excellence, but they are always reluctant to delegate tasks to others. They may suffer from neuritis, sciatica, and skin ailments. The following foods are helpful: apples, strawberries, pineapples, mint, grapes, borage, asparagus, dandelion, sage, peaches, rhubarb, saffron, cloves, nutmeg, almonds, figs, wheat, and hazelnuts. Their twelfth, twenty-first, thirty-ninth, forty-eighth, and fifty-seventh years are turning points in terms of health, and every year they should protect their health during the months of February, June, September and December.

number four These people have a tendency to suffer from mysterious ailments that confound routine diagnosis. They usually complain about headaches, back pain, and melancholia and may suffer from anemia. The lucky foods for these people include spinach, sage, peaches, and plums. They should keep away from highly seasoned or spicy foods and avoid red meat. Number four people respond well to mental suggestion and hypnotism. The years that will show changes in their health are their thirteenth, twenty-second, thirty-first, fortieth, forty-ninth, and fifty-eighth. They should be very careful about their health in the months of January, February, July, August, and September.

number five They tend to overwork their nervous systems, becoming hypersensitive, overwrought, and sleep-deprived through worrying about trivial matters. The most effective medicine for them is sleep and rest. Eating carrots, parsnip, oatmeal, thyme, hazelnuts, walnuts, parsley, and mushrooms is also beneficial. The years that mark changes in the health of number five people are their fourteenth, twenty-third, forty-first, and fiftieth. They should safeguard their health particularly in the months of June, September and December.

number six These people tend to suffer from problems of the nose, throat, and upper respiratory tract. They remain healthy and full of vigor if they live in the country, where there is plenty of fresh air and sunshine. Women with a birth number of six often suffer from breast problems. Many number six people experience heart and circulation problems in later life. People whose birth number is six will benefit from eating any kinds of beans, spinach, mint, melons, squash, figs, almonds, apples, peaches, thyme, pomegranates, and products derived from roses, such as rosewater or jam. The years in which they experience significant health change are their fifteenth, twenty-fourth, forty-second, fifty-first, and sixtieth. They need to be extra careful about their well-being in the months of May, October, and November.

number seven They tend to worry more than others and also often find themselves annoyed or disgruntled. Although in good spirits when the going is good, if they are anxious about people or circumstances at work, they imagine things are worse than they really are, and they sink into self-pity and gloom. Number seven people are sensitive to the vibrations of those around them, and they go to great trouble to please anyone who praises them. They are also able to accomplish those tasks they love, although their bodies may succumb to the pressures of overwork. Another peculiarity of number seven people is their sensitive skin, which is prone to rashes, itching, tenderness, and perspiration. They can improve their health by eating cabbage, lettuce, endive, cucumber, linseed, mushrooms, sorrel, apples, grapes, and all kinds of fruit juices. Their seventh, sixteenth, twenty-fifth, thirty-fourth, forty-third, fifty-second and sixty-first years are eventful. They tend to overwork during the months of January, February, July, and August.

number eight These people have liver, bile, and intestinal problems. They get frequent headaches and may also suffer from rheumatism. They will benefit from eating a vegetarian diet of cereals, vegetables, and pulses, cutting out meat and reducing their consumption of animal products as much as possible. They will especially benefit from eating spinach, carrots, angelica, bananas, celery, and a variety of herbs, including sage and elderflower. Their seventeenth, twenty-sixth, thirty-fifth, forty-fourth, fifty-third, and sixty-second years will show marked changes in their health. They should guard their health in the months of January, February, December, and July, looking for signs of overwork, fatigue, and ill health.

number nine They are generally predisposed to fevers of any kind, measles, or chicken pox. They should keep away from rich or fatty foods and all alcoholic drinks. Number nine people benefit from eating onions, garlic, leeks, rhubarb, mustard seeds, ginger, pepper, nettle juice, and horseradish. Their ninth, eighteenth, twenty-seventh, thirty-sixth, forty-fifth, and sixty-third years mark a change in their health, and the months that may bring overwork or ill health are April, May, October, and November.

Dreams & health

The Hindu belief that man is a microcosm, or the world in miniature, is an ancient one. Just as the world has elements both physical as well as spiritual, so every human being has a soul and a psychic firmament filled with knowledge and deep understanding. By examining our thoughts, each of us can interpret messages received from within ourselves.

Interpreting our dreams is one tool for reading these signals. There are dreams about health and illness that reveal both the present and the future. There are also dreams about apparently unrelated objects or circumstances that can provide similar insights into the state of our health. On the other hand, dreaming about health-related issues does not necessarily point to illness:

abscess If you see yourself with an abscess, you will soon be overwhelmed by your own ill luck, but still sympathetic to the worries of others.

accident This dream warns you not to travel by any kind of transportation for a short while, as you would risk fatality.

adversary If you dream of meeting an adversary, sickness may engulf you. If you overpower the adversary, some serious misfortune will be averted.

ax Seeing a rusty ax foretells illness as well as the loss of wealth and property.

back Seeing a bare back is indicative of sickness.

baking If a woman sees herself baking, she must be careful of her health and of the children that she looks after.

ball If you see yourself alone at a ball or party, there may a death in the family quite soon after.

87

bath For a pregnant woman to dream of taking a bath foretells the possibility of miscarriage or accident. A warm bath is usually connected with something evil.

bed If you dream of wetting your bed, sickness or tragedy in business will follow.

blood Seeing blood on your hands forewarns of immediate bad luck. To see bleeding means that you will confront people who are spreading false stories about you.

boils If you see boils on your forehead, someone close to you may fall sick.

bones A pile of bones denotes bad influences that surround you.

crying baby This dream denotes ill health with disappointments to follow.

doctor This is a good omen, denoting good health and prosperity.

fireworks This dream denotes wonderful health to come.

gangrene This forewarns of the death of a parent or close relative.

heart To see your own heart is a warning of sickness and fatigue.

hives To see your child affected by hives means that it will be very healthy.

illness If a woman dreams of her own illness, an unforseen event will toss her into a frenzy of nervous tension, and she will miss a much-awaited visit or amusement.

invalid To dream of invalids shows that your detractors will try to harm your interest.

itch If you see yourself itching, you will be blamed for something and will find a way out by casting aspersions on others.

jaundice If you see yourself with jaundice, you will flourish after initial failures.

madness To dream of madness shows that sickness, through which you could lose property, is likely.

medicine If you dream of a pleasant-tasting medicine, what seems like a bad period in your life will soon work in your favor. If you see a bitter medicine, you will suffer a long illness or will have to face some deep sorrow.

owl If you hear the cry of an owl, illness or death will approach you even while you enjoy good health. A dead owl denotes a narrow escape from a great illness.

peaches Seeing or eating peaches foretells the sickness of children. Eating pears also shows approaching ill health.

peas Eating peas shows that bursting good health is just around the corner.

pregnancy If a woman is actually pregnant and sees herself thus in a dream, she will have a safe delivery.

sickness This usually foretells a real sickness in the family.

sore throat This denotes that you will be unhappy about your judgment after a friend deceives you.

skeleton This dream warns of illness or injury at the hands of others. If you see yourself as one, you have been worrying unnecessarily about an issue that has a simple solution. If one haunts you, be very careful, for a grave accident may await you.

storm To see a storm or hear it approaching means that you are in for a period of prolonged illness, during which you will be parted from friends. If the storm passes by, the problem will not be acute.

Astrology & health

E ach sign of the zodiac is associated with a planet. Every planet has characteristics that influence our health, knowledge of which enables us to piece together our unique health profiles.

If you have had your horoscope compiled by an astrologer, you will see that it is divided into twelve sections, or houses. The eighth house reveals health problems that can lead to death, although a detailed reading is required. If your eighth house contains the following signs, you must safeguard yourself from the following accidents and ailments:

aquarius fever, asthma, delirium, ailments of the heart, consumption

pisces elephantiasis, water-related accidents and complaints

aries fever, indigestion and gastric troubles

taurus throat trouble, inflammation of the lungs, injury from weapons

gemini stomach ulcers, kidney failure, diseases of the lungs

cancer meningitis, problems related to the kidneys or liver, gastric troubles

leo boils, fevers of all kinds, animal bites, especially those of dogs, or attacks by enemies

virgo sexual diseases, an accidental fall from a height

libra fever, typhoid, meningitis, malaria, or diseases of the brain

scorpio diphtheria, liver and kidney disorders, anemia, or dysentry

sagittarius injury from lethal weapons, accidental fall from a height, water-related calamities

capricorn diseases of the brain

Palmistry & health

Refer to pages
56–61 for
descriptions
of the lines
and mounts of
the palm.

The ancient study of the hand, its lines, mounts, and hollows, can give powerful indication of a person's character, as well as the influences acting on his or her health. Of the many lines that crisscross over our palms, one line runs from the base of the palm from the center of the wrist toward the base of the little finger in a gently curved diagonal. This is the line of health, also called the Hepatica. This line should be as straight as possible, as a straight line indicates a life of good health. However, an absence of this line indicates excellent health.

Certain features in the line of health reveal health problems to guard against. If the line of health is broad and faint, the individual will have circulatory problems. If it is very bright red, this indicates heart trouble. An intermittently dark and light line of health indicates a tendency toward fever. When the line twists and looks crooked, biliousness and liver complaints are sure to affect the individual. A line that is broken in places indicates poor digestion.

The line of health must be read in conjunction with the nails, mounts and other lines on the palm. If consisting of little islands and found in conjunction with long nails, the line of health reveals that the lungs and chest will cause problems, while smaller islands coupled with long nails indicate throat ailments. If the line of health arrives at the mount of

Mercury, the raised portion of the hand at the base of the little finger, there is the risk of a weak heart. If it intersects the line of life, which curves in an arc from about 1 inch below the index finger toward the wrist, this is a general indication of dangerous health. When the line of health is contained within the line of heart (running along the top of the palm beneath the fingers) and the line of head and touches both of them, there is a danger of mental weakness.

The bracelets

These are the lines that run around the wrist at the base of the palm. The first bracelet nearest to the palm is connected with health. When this ring is high into the palm and even enters the palm in an arc, it warns of a weakness in the internal organs. In women, this can reveal a difficulty in conceiving or bearing children. Such people are advised to heed their bodies' early warnings to heal themselves quickly.

Islands

Islands, or a series of loops, on any line are not a good sign. On the line of life, they foretell illnesses or low resistance. On the line of head, they show a hereditary tendency toward mental instability. In both cases, the point where the islands occur indicates the age at which the individual will become unwell.

The nails

The nails offer an accurate indication of one's health. If they are especially long, lung or chest ailments will occur, and if the nails are curved, these ailments will be particularly serious. Ribbed nails are a sign of physical weakness and chronic ill health. Short, ribbed nails denote throat problems such as laryngitis or bronchitis. Nails that are bluish in color suggest a sluggish circulation and are most often seen in women. If the nails are small and short they indicate heart trouble. If somewhat sunken into the flesh, they reveal nervous ailments. Short nails that curve upward at the edges may be warning of the danger of paralysis. It is a general rule of palmistry that shorter-nailed people tend to have problems with the heart and the lower body, whereas longer-nailed people suffer from problems of the upper body. Many people have nails that are flecked with white spots, which signifies a highly nervous disposition.

Our hands provide clues regarding our health. If these are heeded, we can take preventive measures and reduce the chance of serious ill health.

Family

Where fools are not adored
The food grains are properly stored
The husband and wife do not clash
There graces "Sri" of her own accord.

Chanakya's *Neeti Shastra* about Sri, Goddess of Fortune (c. 350–275 B.C.)

There was time, not long ago, when families lived together. Growing economies now compel us to travel farther from home, and many of us feel we have drifted away from those we love the most. We are often too far from our families to help in times of crisis, and due to the stresses of modern living, when reunited with our loved ones, we tend to argue more than we hug. Ideally, whether we live apart or together, we should enjoy peaceful, envy-free relationships with all our family members.

The most important quality, absent from many modern-day homes, is a sense of belonging. In the past, Indian families lived together, providing social and economic support for all of their members. Today, the closed, extended family has all but disappeared. Individuals wander away in search of employment or education, and the small, nuclear family is left to fend for itself.

Which of us would not want greater understanding to reign within our home? However, this requires effort and a willingness to meet others halfway. Keeping a good relationship alive or rejuvenating an ailing one can be helped by some of the luck tools that are explained in this book. Some of us need luck to understand our parents better, for our children to emerge as winners in the race of life, for our brothers and sisters to be healthy and prosperous or even for our spouses to give us the gift of friendship and consideration. Humans cannot live in isolation, and therefore it is imperative that healthy relationships be fed and watered with the nectar of love and luck.

Gems & the family

For centuries people have worn gems in order to benefit from the gems' ability to increase vitality and to counteract negative influences. Some gems are particularly useful in family situations, as they can help people to remain calm and assess situations before they react. The vibrations that certain stones emit can encourage the wearer to remain generous and forgiving, loving and supportive. These are all qualities that we need in abundance when we wish to nurture a fruitful relationship.

red gems If you are facing a confusing situation in your family life and are unsure of what will make everyone happy, try wearing a pink gem such as rose quartz. This will help focus your emotions and enable you to decide on a course of action. Rose quartz is also a popular choice because of the feelings of forgiveness and unconditional love that it promotes. In the modern world, these are qualities that are almost mantras for busy parents with growing children. Rose quartz will help parents cope calmly with the pressures of parenthood.

orange gems Stones such as amber and coral harmonize the emotions and help us deal with them effectively. Wear an orange stone if you are stuck in a deadlock situation with a relative. Your obstinate refusal to forgive and forget may just melt away, allowing you to enjoy a worthwhile relationship once more. Many women bring a feeling of self-pity or a lack of self- 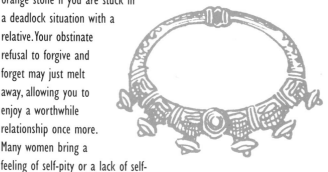 esteem into a marriage. Wearing an orange stone will dissipate these feelings and make a woman more able to form an equal relationship with her spouse. Amber also absorbs depression and feelings of negativity.

yellow gems This is the color of confidence. Yellow gems such as topaz and citrine affect the nervous system, cleansing it of negative vibrations, so that we can be carefree and joyful. These stones make us feel confident in a group, so that we are able to bring light and laughter to family outings or gatherings.

green gems The color green helps to overcome envy and possessiveness. Emeralds or jade can help you to detach yourself from a partner, providing breathing space within the relationship. No marriage can survive the asphyxiation of suspicion and domination. A green gem will give you the calm self-assurance you need to overcome these negative feelings, so that your relationship can develop in an environment of mutual freedom and support. Emeralds are particularly recommended for enhancing one's powers of communication. If your relationship is in the doldrums, due to unspoken misunderstandings or prolonged silences, wear an emerald in order to open up the channels of dialogue.

blue gems The color blue gives us the strength to take control of the people and situations around us. If keeping your family together is your goal, you already know that each member has to be responsible for the others. Stones such as sapphires, aquamarines, turquoise, blue topaz, and lapis lazuli inspire thoughts of acceptance and generosity in us, so that we are more inclined to work toward the good of the family. Blue gems are particularly helpful if you sense that feelings of selfishness and secretiveness are taking hold of you, preventing you from enjoying a happy familial relationship.

purple gems This is the color of spirituality and change. We find that with each passing generation, there are changes in the values we all live by. Some of us find it difficult to accept these changes and cling to old patterns of thought and behavior. This can be distressing for others, especially children, who are the owners of a bright, new world unfettered by rigid traditions. If you feel unable to turn your thoughts toward modernity, try wearing an amethyst. This will help you look objectively at new thoughts and values and will strengthen your relationships with younger people.

white gems This is the color of introspection. A good relationship with a parent, sibling, child, or spouse can easily turn sour when each person sticks to his or her own notions of what is right. Wearing a white gem, such as a pearl, will help you look within yourself to determine and accept your own faults first, and to correct these before blaming others. Pearls are also said to augur a happy married life, and Indian brides wear them to ensure future happiness and prevent sudden widowhood.

Other white gems, such as diamonds and transparent crystals, enhance confidence and leadership. If you feel that a family situation can be nudged toward success, wear a white gem to give yourself the courage and commitment to take charge and move toward your goals.

black gems This color offers protection from evil. Wear smoky quartz or jet if you need a protective armor against a jealous or petty relative. The gem will help deflect these negative vibrations while teaching you detachment and the art of finding joy in life's great variety.

Color & the family

Every color has a unique set of vibrations which affect the way we feel. Given this fact, the colors we wear reveal our personalities (how we deal with people and situations), and by choosing these colors carefully, we can bring greater luck into our lives. Depending upon your situation, one of the following colors can make you more open toward building better relationships with your family.

red Wear red if you are going to put forward a proposal to your family. This color will help you present the idea in a convincing way, and, assuming your plans are reasonable, it will encourage your family to agree with what you have to say. Conversely, if you are tense or worried about your plans, do not wear red, as this will convey your nervous energy to your relatives, who may then subconsciously reject what you are saying. Also, if you recognize the tendency within yourself to become angry quickly, avoid wearing red during family discussions. This color will make confrontation impossible to avoid, resulting in a wasted opportunity both for the exchange of ideas and the agreeing on a compromise.

pink This is the color to wear when you are nurturing a sick or anxious relative. Pink makes you sympathetic to the woes of older people or the constant fretting of little children. Deep shades of pink enhance your feelings of selfless love, so that you become more caring and giving. However, never wear pink if you are in need of emotional support yourself. If you are feeling under pressure while looking after the young or old, pink will make you feel nervous and inadequate.

orange Wear orange when humor needs to be injected into a family situation, perhaps when a parent or spouse has gotten over a serious illness or when a disagreement between siblings has been resolved. This is the color of joy and fun and will lift the depression from somber, heavy situations. However, if you are confused about how to resolve the problem with your sibling, or if you are frustrated about your own inability to find a solution, wearing orange will deepen your anxieties and sense of helplessness. Also, if you feel suffocated by your husband or wife, orange will add to your worries, as it also represents claustrophobia.

yellow In every family there are occasions when aunts, uncles, cousins, or siblings create unpleasant situations in which one member must judge how to settle matters amicably. If you find yourself in this difficult position, wear yellow. The color of impartial, detached thinking, it will help you reach a reasonable decision. You will also be able to persuade both parties to follow the course you have plotted. This advice is particularly relevant if a dispute has arisen from deep misunderstandings. However, if you are afraid of others' disapproval or unwilling to accept their criticism, yellow will demoralize you further.

green This is the color of plenty. Nature is green, and everyone is touched by its abundance and generosity. Wear green if you are in a situation that requires your patience and understanding. Green will make you appealing to children, who will sense your calm participation in their emotions. Siblings will be grateful for your helpful attitude, and parents will appreciate the faith you place in them. Green is the essence of new beginnings and optimism, so if things have been low and dismal with your spouse, a touch of green will help infuse fresh hope into the relationship. Never wear green if you need to be active and make a decision quickly.

Do not attempt to resolve family problems when dressed in green, because this color delays rapid action and quick outcomes. Instead, you will find that the problems linger with no immediate solution in sight.

blue There are times in our life when we feel overwhelmed by our problems, whether they be demanding relatives or noisy children, the pressures of juggling several relationships at once, or feeling that one is all things to all people. We would do well to wear blue at such times, especially as it is the color of introspection and relaxation. Wear blue if you are looking for a period of isolation while you take stock of a family situation.

On the other hand, do not wear blue if you are feeling lonely and depressed because of a particular relationship, as this color will enhance the feelings of isolation and misery and will not help you to resolve any differences or make the first move toward a solution.

purple All shades of purple, from eggplant to lavender, promote inner peace. Wear this color for focusing your inner energies toward healing your relationships. It will give you the clarity and constancy of purpose, coupled with an aura of peace, to deal with any distressing situation. It will also provide the sensitivity required to appreciate the efforts of your family toward making your life easy and happy. On the negative side, wearing purple will increase feelings of oversensitivity if your emotions have taken a recent battering. If you are very young and feel restricted by family rules, duties, and obligations, purple will make you feel unduly pressurized.

white White is a color of quiet waiting. If you are in a situation where it is better to stand by and watch the family cope alone, this is the color you should wear. Even in a celebration, such as a wedding, wearing white affirms your presence and support without your having to proclaim it. Do not wear white if your participation in a decision-making process within the family is crucial. Your loved ones will view your inaction as aloof or even arrogant. If you must wear white, add a dash of yellow to enhance your skills of communication, or orange to spur you into action.

black Have you been in a situation where your family members are trying to influence you regarding a decision about your own life, especially when you have already made up your mind? Well, wearing black will help you maintain your position without offending others. It will give you an aura of authority and self-assurance, so that your family will be more willing to accept your decision. Keep away from black if your siblings or spouse do not seem to respect you. In this case, black will enhance your feeling of low self-esteem and depress you further.

Symbols & the family

Indians love decoration in every form, and everything from a truck to the floor of a rural dwelling becomes a candidate for embellishment. Their fascination with color, form, and pattern has enabled ancient symbols, both artistic and spiritual, to retain their meaning and popular appeal. Traditional Indian symbols range from ornaments to gestures, and one of the most enduring is an action of surrender. All Hindu children are taught to touch the feet of their elders during special occasions, and the custom of bowing before those who are older or wiser continues into adulthood.

Tree of Life

One of the symbols used to enhance a family's luck is the tree of life. Symbolic of the family and its interdependence, the tree of life pattern flourished under the Mogul rule in India. This motif originated in the verdant, flower-laden valleys of Kashmir, where nature provided endless inspiration for the creation of design. The creeper—round, sinuous, and sensual—was copied from the myriad gardens of Kashmir and gives an impetus to the tree of life. The motif uses intertwined creepers, leaves, cones, and jewel-hued flowers to create an ascending pattern. Frolicking among the foliage of this stylized tree are birds with exotic plumes, giving the motif movement and energy. In other interpretations, the tree of life is embellished with paisley motifs and fruit.

This motif also has a deep psychic meaning. It is sometimes used to depict the cycle of life, in which all life forms are sustained through their beauty and usefulness. The endless creepers represent support. The birds speak of joy, music, and freedom, each contributing individually to the good of the whole. The flowers symbolize change and progress, and, as they grow in the same direction as the tree, they also represent family. The tree of life motif is contained within a given space, symbolizing the discipline and rules within which we must function in order to belong to a greater whole.

It is easy to understand why the tree of life motif should signify luck for the family. It stands for everything a family should be. You can easily create your own tree of life by including your favorite leaves and flowers. Give drawings of these to all your relatives as a constant reminder that it is only by working toward the common good of all that a family can be strong and united.

Rakhi

Another means of attracting good luck is for a sister to tie a decorative colored thread, called a *rakhi*, to her brother's right-hand wrist. The brother pledges to protect her in return, and this bond of love is strengthened each year. This ritual has its own festival, Raksha Bandhan, which falls in the monsoon, when the rains create a symphony for peacocks to dance to. While the *rakhi* has become a powerful symbol of brotherly duty and love, women also tie threads to men whose goodwill and friendship they seek.

One of the origins of this custom can be traced back to the great Indian epic the *Mahabharata*. In one chapter, Krishna hurts his finger while throwing a discus at a villain. Queen Draupadi, the beautiful heroine of the story, is standing close by and hastily tears a strip of cloth from her scarf. She rushes to Krishna and ties the makeshift bandage around his bloody finger. Krishna pledges that in return for her kindness, he will protect her when she needs him. Later in the story, Krishna becomes Draupadi's savior when she is dishonored at court.

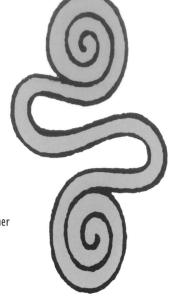

Metals & the family

Indians believe that wearing certain metals can increase one's chances of enjoying lucky family relationships. We know that each metal is governed by a planet and imbued with its qualities, both positive and negative. If you are aware of problems in your relationships with your parents, siblings, spouse, or children, or even if you want simply to strengthen these relationships, try wearing whichever of these metals is appropriate:

gold If you are oversensitive and take offense easily, or if you feel that you are the butt of family jokes, wear gold to counteract these emotions. In a confrontation with a loved one, it is all too easy to flare up in anger and drive that person away. Gold will temper your impulsiveness and neutralize any feelings of confusion. You will also be able to listen to a spouse or sibling with a sympathetic ear, which will fortify your relationship. Also, if there is a need to resolve family problems in which you are not directly involved, wear gold to reduce obstacles and prepare the way for others to create compromise.

silver Are you the kind of person who always forgets birthdays, wedding anniversaries, or other days special to the family? Are you forever in a rush to buy a last-minute card or gift for your spouse, siblings, or parents? If all this sounds familiar, then you also know the embarrassment you feel and the look you receive from a disappointed relative when he or she receives your belated card or gift. Remembering and acknowledging a special day in the life of a loved one is an important way of letting that person know how much you care. A parent, brother, or sister will love you for remembering, especially if you live a long way away. According to Indian metal science, silver is ruled by Jupiter, whose influence makes people meticulous and sharp. Jupiter is the planet of wisdom and caring and governs memory as well. If you want to banish forgetfulness, wear silver in the form of a ring, bracelet, or chain. If you believe with all your heart, Jupiter can help to make you seem like the most sensitive person in your family.

Silver is also associated with the Moon. If you are a timid, helpful, and kind person, but with a mind that is easily swayed by what you hear, or if you cannot face family disputes directly, silver is the metal for you. Wear it if you cannot discriminate between right and wrong, or if you are in a situation where you have to stand up for what is right.

copper There is a tendency in many of us to be too frank and outspoken in the belief that we are simply being honest. This bluntness is often the cause of family rifts or misunderstandings. Ruffled feelings, which could just as easily be smoothed by kind, diplomatic words, can be upset even further by brutal frankness. The family should be a reliable source of support, always there to hold a relative's hand through troubled times. An honest but discreet appraisal of each situation, followed by advice that lifts the spirits, will always be appreciated. If you are an outspoken person and feel the need to cultivate caution and thoughtfulness, wearing copper will help.

The quality of stubbornness, which prevents good relationships from changing and growing, can also be tempered by wearing copper. If you are someone who becomes increasingly adamant when you feel imposed upon, copper will help you become reasonable and understanding.

iron We have all met people who impose their will on others in the belief that they are being helpful or that what they say is correct. As parents they tend to control their children, as spouses they dominate their partner, and as siblings they take life too seriously and assume too much responsibility for the destinies of others. Such people would do well to carry an iron object on their person. This could be a key or a key chain which will enhance their ability to let go. Iron also allows them to be sympathetic to older people, and with this metal on their person, they will be young at heart however old they grow. Iron will also help them to receive their relatives' love and care and find comfort in the nurturing of a spouse.

Vastu shastra & the family

Vastu Shastra has evolved over thousands of years and encompasses engineering, interior and exterior design, astronomy, and earth sciences, teaching us to create the ideal environment for balance and harmony within the home. According to this ancient science, a house is divided into eight portions, each governed by a particular direction.

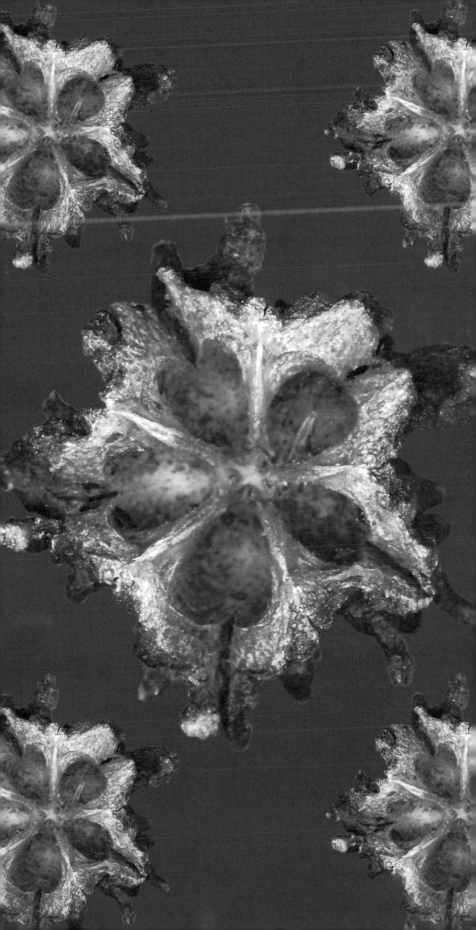

The luck of the family, as well the quality of relationships between family members, depends largely on the location and decor of the kitchen. This is because traditionally it was in the kitchen that the family gathered to cook, eat, and spend time with each other. The interaction of the elements, of wind, water, fire, earth, and space, is most apparent in the kitchen, and a balance of these elements will ensure happiness in the home.

The ideal location for a kitchen is in the southeast corner of the home, because this direction is governed by Agni, the god of fire and heat. Kitchens facing other directions will draw influences into the home environment, affecting the luck and happiness of the family:

north Children will be intelligent. The family will be financially secure.

northeast There will always be over-spending and mental unrest for the entire family.

northwest The family will spend more than it earns and, as a consequence, be extremely stressed.

east The lady of the house will be unhappy despite all comforts and will transfer her misery to the people around her.

southeast Ideal. This will bring luck and happiness.

south Family fights and unrest.

southwest Illness and depression will affect everyone in the house.

west Although the women of the house will be happy, there will be an undercurrent of friction among family members.

the kitchen layout To promote fulfillment and togetherness within the home, arrange the kitchen as follows:

If it is not possible for the kitchen to be in the southeast corner, the oven should be placed in the southeast corner of the kitchen.

It is best to cook facing the east or the south, but never looking toward the north or the west.

All cooking utensils should be kept facing south or southwest.

It is best if faucets are placed in the northeast corner of the kitchen.

The food-storage cabinet should be situated in the southwest of the kitchen. It will be even more beneficial if there is a solid door that shields the contents from view.

Where the kitchen is also used for eating, the table should be kept in the western corner. The refrigerator should be sited in the northwest of the kitchen.

Other parts of the house also affect the family:

If the steps that lead up to a house are broken or badly worn, the household expenditure will supersede the income, and the man of the house will bring home all the frustrations of his work.

If the façade of the house, meaning the exterior walls of the front of the house, is damaged by cracks or if the paint is peeling, the lady of the house will be restless and unable to contribute to the progress of the family.

If there are rocks or dying plants at the front of the house, the family income will be earned after great hardship. The family will borrow money constantly and face the embarrassment of unpaid debts, causing the man of the house unbearable tension.

If there is a barber shop, a goldsmith's, or a laundry adjacent to the house, happiness cannot reside there.

A dilapidated house or one with a lake opposite is unlucky, as the man of the house will be dissatisfied and will wander in body and spirit.

Pillars built within the house that are in line with the main door are inauspicious. The family will never enjoy mutual cooperation or understanding, and there will be great rivalry among the inhabitants.

Always keep the main bedroom neat and beautifully decorated, as this will ensure that the lady of the house will be in constant good spirits.

Pay great attention to the beauty of your front door. A beautiful, well-maintained door invites good fortune.

Numbers & the family

In numerology, special meaning is attached to the number derived from the date of a person's birth. This is called the birth number. Each birth number contains psychic vibrations that influence our personalities and our luck. To calculate your birth number, simply add together the numbers of the day you were born (for example, a person born on the twenty-seventh of a month will have the birth number nine). This number represents different qualities, which affect how a person interacts with his or her family. Understanding one's birth number enables one to enhance relationships within the home:

number one This is the number of the Sun and therefore of the basis of all life. A person born under this number is highly individual; this can be

used effectively to steer one's family toward good times. However, a number one person can also be obstinate and should try to be flexible if relationships are to be congenial. These traits are found in all those born on the first, tenth, nineteenth, or twenty-eighth of any month, but more particularly if they are born between July twenty-first and August twenty-eighth. This is because it is the zodiac period called the House of the Sun. People born between March twenty-first and April twenty-eighth will demonstrate these qualities even more acutely, as this is the period when the Sun enters the vernal equinox and is considered all-powerful.

number two These people are symbolically governed by the Moon. They can be restless and unsettled if they are not occupied and tend to bring nervous tension into the home. They look to the family for their sense of well-being and become despondent if the home is not a cheerful place. They are inclined to draw the family into their black moods. They must learn to overcome their dependency on a spouse or parent and to search for happiness within themselves.

number three If you are a number three person, you know that you detest being obliged to anyone. In fact, you are so proud that when your family offers you help, you decline their offer. You hate restraint and believe in your ability to be independently happy. However, it is obvious that our happiness depends to an extent on those around us; therefore it is essential that you allow your family to take some responsibility for your emotional well-being.

number four A number four person tends to look at everything differently from other people. Although they do not mean to be antagonistic, they frequently cause people around them to be confrontational. Number four people need to extinguish the bright flame of rebellion that burns within them and put to rest the urge to create their own set of opposing rules for the entire family. Number fours can, however, infuse a fresh burst of energy into set patterns of behavior that have become established for the family.

number five This is the number of friendship, and number five people get along with almost everyone. They have a resilient nature and spring back easily from the worst personal calamities. It is because of these traits that number five people make excellent counselors, and they are quick to solve any problem within the family. Having said this, number five people are also mentally agile and unable to endure fools gladly. By improving their patience, they can improve family relationships.

number six These people are loyal to a fault and seem to attract everyone around them. If wealthy, they are generous toward their relatives and will fill the home with color and joy. However, number six people should allow other family members to express themselves and their individuality without overshadowing them with their own personality.

number seven All number seven people love to travel and are constantly making plans for the family to visit far-off lands. Their restless natures love change and they include their loved ones in their fantastic dreams. Women born under this number tend to marry well, since they worry about their own future. Number seven people are also deeply involved in mysticism and the occult sciences, and these individuals have a magnetic quality that influences other family members.

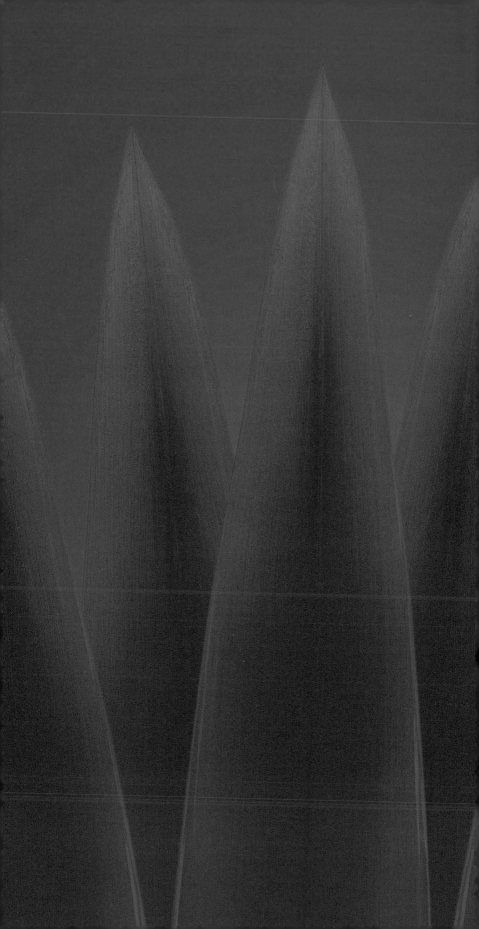

number eight This is symbolically the number of the planet Saturn. People born under this number are not considered fortunate in the realm of personal happiness. They are generally misunderstood by their close relatives throughout their life and are therefore very lonely at heart. They are seen as cold and undemonstrative, although they are not, but they seldom correct this misconception. If the number eight occurs with the number four, e.g. a man born on the fourth whose wife was born on the thirteenth $(4+1+3=8)$, it is wise to be cautious in all dealings with the family, as the fates will so strongly oppose happiness that the entire family may be disrupted. If you have a number eight in the family, you must try your best to make them feel loved and wanted.

number nine This number belongs to the planet Mars. These people are generally hasty and impulsive in speech and action, causing great distress in their personal lives as a result. They have a quarrelsome home life, and do not get along with certain members of the family, either their own or the family they marry into. Number nine people hate being criticized and love to have everything their own way. If they are not indulged, they tend to disregard other people and cause them pain. Number nine people must address the reality of life and think carefully before saying hurtful things.

The first letter of your name

Astro-numerology attaches great importance to the name of an individual. The vibrations created by chanting your name can affect your destiny. These vibrations influence your personality and emotional reactions and can be used to maximize your good fortune. By knowing the traits that endear you to people and those that antagonize them, you can discover how to keep alive your family's love.

A You are openminded and devoted to your family. You will generally be closer to your maternal relatives and feel tenderness toward all family members of the opposite sex. You need to control your impulsiveness in order to listen to your loved ones and offer them help.

B You love beauty and take joy in creating a lovely home and garden. You are sincere in your feelings toward your family. If you are a woman, your attachment to your mother may be resented by your husband or in-laws. You can be difficult to please and need to let go of some of your inflexibility.

C You are energetic and believe in the dictum that variety is the spice of life. You may have problems in marriage due to this. You also need to heed the advice of elders instead of discovering everything for yourself. This will get you into a great deal of trouble.

D You believe in unselfish service and will go out of your way to look after your family. However if you are frustrated in any aspect of your life, you become restless and stingy and are prone to wasting time or gossiping about others.

E You are fond of speed and adventure and should take care not to be hasty or irresponsible toward your relatives. When young, you tend to infuse everything you do with a sexual intensity, which does not necessarily result in actual gratification.

F You are outspoken and will sometimes alienate your loved ones because of it. You are often argumentative and readily offer help and advice even when it is uninvited. You need to use your time judiciously and attend to priorities first.

G You are intelligent and hardworking but also obstinate and secretive. You must learn to give in to others and be open with your family to avoid misunderstandings.

H You are popular and enjoy your family's support. You sometimes become depressed if changes are forced on you, but these should be looked at as blessings in disguise.

I You are very attached to your family and take your responsibilities seriously. You should, however, tone down your oversensitivity and refrain from being critical toward your family members, as they make many sacrifices on your behalf. Also never brood over the past, as this will ruin the present.

J You are charitable and jolly and love your independence. Be careful not to hurt the feelings of your relatives and in-laws by being overly self-sufficient. Use your natural optimism to keep the family's spirits high.

K You are very involved in domestic matters and would do well to let the family be. Watching constantly over your loved ones can cause rivalry and envy. Use your intelligence for the greater good of the world.

L You dislike taking the advice of others, and if you are not as successful in your career as you would like to be, you secretly blame your parents for it. You suffer from a superiority complex. You generally marry early in life and have an attractive, well-kept home.

M You seek the company of older relatives, so that you can learn from their experience. You must overcome your inflexibility and pessimism to have a happy family life. When young, you face separation from your loved ones.

N You have a highly active mind and become easily frustrated if things do not happen as you want them to. You need to control your ego and learn to appreciate the value and noble qualities of others. You rarely compromise your principles and generally repeat your mistakes. Learn to accept your faults and heed the advice of others.

O You have a wavering mind. You also love to meddle in the affairs of others, and if your views are not accepted, you change the subject and start a new discussion. Use your interest in spirituality to calm your soul.

P You are thoughtful and perfect in manners and grooming. You hate being apart from your loved ones, and divorce is anathema to you. You may enjoy somewhat too much alcohol, and this will put a strain on the family.

Q You have high expectations that your family will find hard to live up to. You love the outdoors and will often be away from home. Although you are usually frank, you seem to conceal vital information. Learn to be realistic in your hopes and open in your affections.

R You tend to gain respect within your family as you advance in age. You are able to adjust to the needs of your family but need to beware of those close to you who may take advantage of your weaknesses or secrets and harass you.

S You are outgoing and gregarious but need to listen to the advice of your elders when important decisions about your own life are concerned. This is because you tend to be confused and might make the wrong choice. Use your social skills to please the family.

T You possess a suspicious streak in your otherwise generous nature. You love relating your experiences to your family, and dinnertime is made all the more lively by your stories. However, you become oversensitive and upset when considered imperfect by your loved ones. Your old age is generally emotionally stable.

U You tend to spend long periods away from home, but you are very attached to your children. Your behavior is sometimes seen as childish, and maturity comes to you late in life. However, women with this personality type are a great support to their husbands and never shun their obligations.

V You are considerate and generous and create a party atmosphere in the home. You carry the burden of the entire family, helping in whatever way you can, but harbor many imaginary fears that exasperate your loved ones.

W You are aggressive and should control your need to dominate your family. You are undemonstrative and may appear harsh. You tend to have secret relationships, although these do not damage your home life. Women with this personality type should resist the urge to overspend the family budget.

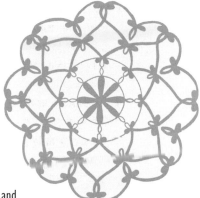

X You are emotional and make sacrifices for your family. However you have a streak of sarcasm and can be quite moody. You need to stop daydreaming and face any family problems head on. Make an effort to appear cheerful.

Y You can be quite self-centered and tend to get overwrought about minor quarrels in the household. You should use your aptitude for social work to keep busy. This will ensure that you are not idle for long.

Z You are a puzzle to your loved ones and you enjoy that. However, you love your home and family and try to make exciting plans for them. When young, you should guard against appearing too smug and brash with your relatives.

Dreams & the family

All dreams contain messages about our waking lives. By understanding the significance of our dreams, we can deal more effectively with all aspects of our lives. Dreams always point to the future, and at times they are so vivid that the messages they contain are immediately apparent. Here are some dreams that relate specifically to the family:

father To dream of your father denotes that you are about to face some difficulty and that you will need some wise advice in order to overcome it. If you see your father dead, this indicates that you should exercise caution in business. If a young woman dreams of her dead father, her lover will probably stray in the near future.

father-in-law To see your father-in-law in good spirits means that you will enjoy good family relations.

mother To see your mother in her home means that you will find success in a new project. If you are conversing with her, you will receive news that you were anxiously awaiting. If your mother is dead or dying, there will be sorrow or dishonor in your future. If your mother calls out to you, you are making a wrong career move.

mother-in-law This dream signifies happy reunions after a quarrel. If a young woman sees herself quarreling with her mother-in-law, she will shortly encounter uncaring people.

son If you dream of a good son, and if you really have one, he will make you proud. To see him ill or disfigured means that you will experience difficulty.

daughter To see your daughter means that unpleasant events will transform into harmony and peace. If she disobeys you, you will be restless and miserable.

daughter-in-law There will be an unusual experience in your life which will be pleasant or unpleasant, depending on whether your daughter-in-law is friendly or disagreeable.

children If an unmarried woman dreams of giving birth to a baby, she can expect a fall from honor in some area of her life. If you see many children playing happily, you will encounter very good fortune; this is a very lucky dream indeed. If they are studying or working, general happiness in the home will follow. To see your child very ill or even dead is a dangerous dream, as your child may be in very grave danger.

brother If your brothers are seen rejoicing, there will be a stroke of good luck in their lives or yours. If they are begging or financially insecure, a death or a great tragedy may befall you or them.

aunt If a young woman sees her aunt, she will be bitterly reprimanded for an action of hers. If the aunt seems happy, minor skirmishes in the family will soon be resolved.

uncle To see your uncle foretells unpleasant news. If you see your uncle dead, you should beware of hidden enemies. To quarrel with your uncle shows that there will be estrangement and illness in the family.

cousin To see one's cousins shows pending failures and problems. If you write a letter to your cousin, a distressing parting of ways will occur within the family.

grandparents If you see yourself talking to grandparents, you will meet obstacles that will be difficult to overcome, but you may find a solution if you take the advice of more experienced people.

husband If you see your husband happy and prosperous, your home life will be peaceful. If he is sick or tired, a member of the family will require your care and attention to recover from an illness. If you see him leaving you for no reason, a quarrel may be imminent, but this will be resolved quickly. If he is suspicious of you, in reality he will trust you but other troubles will arise. If your husband is seen in love with another woman, he will talk of needing a change and will seem restless. If he is killed while he is with another woman, there is danger of losing your property, and a calamity will follow.

yourself To see yourself in love with someone else's husband indicates that you are unhappy in your marriage and that there is no immediate scope for happiness. If your are an unmarried woman and you dream of being married, you consider yourself lacking in the womanly qualities that men seek.

wife To see your wife signifies tension in the home. If she is very romantic toward you, you will create an unexpected profit for your business.

stepsister You will have the responsibility of looking after someone thrust upon you.

family To see one's family happy signifies good health and fortune. If there is sorrow, depression will follow.

nephew/niece To see your nephew looking handsome is lucky, and you will soon receive good news. If he is ill, you will be troubled by minor worries. If a woman dreams of her niece, she will have to face sudden disappointments or illness.

Astrology & the family

Every horoscope is divided into twelve houses, and these govern a person's life. The third house is that of relatives. It tells us about brothers, sisters, family environment, relationships, and the mentality of the individual. The seventh house is that of marriage, and it determines the degree of happiness that the person will derive from his or her marriage and partnerships. The fourth house is that of the home, and it signifies the father and mother, one's childhood, old age, inherited characteristics, and one's acquisition or inheritance of property. To discover the secrets of your horoscope, you will need to visit an astrologer. However, each sign of the zodiac has particular characteristics which influence the way we lead our lives.

aquarius A man born under the sign of Aquarius is cool but vibrantly electric. He seems to have no time for emotions, and yet his family loves his energy and love of life. His planet rules the unexpected, so he can be unpredictable and oscillate between extremes of good and bad. A woman born under this sign does not rely on feminine wiles and manipulation in marriage. Instead she brings a steadfast loyalty and an open appreciation of her partner's  achievements. She is also a paradox, as she remains detached from her loved ones but willing to do almost anything for them.

pisces This is a very spiritual man, always interested in discovering the sacred space of his inner self. He appreciates depth and intelligence in his family and is unlikely to want to spend Friday night out on the town. He would rather read a book on tarot or take a course in meditation, even if it means spending less time with his loved ones. Pisces woman loves feeling protected. She can endure hardships in life, but they take their toll, and she soon realizes that beyond her dream world there exists a real one full of harsh truths and imperfect reflections. She constantly expects her family to achieve an impossible ideal and therefore becomes dejected often.

aries You are maddeningly honest, so much so that sometimes your family wants to shake you into saying something that they want to hear. Try to listen and agree occasionally. Women sometimes seek to excel in traditionally male-dominated areas, thereby ruffling a few conservative feathers. Keep up the good work, but don't show off. Instead use your extraordinary resilience to keep the family going from strength to strength.

taurus You love luxury and style and can seem lazy to those around you. Try to work as hard as you play. Your sense of fun is apparent when you make quicksilver plans for family picnics or trips to the movies, but your loved ones may find themselves breathless trying to keep pace. Taurus

women have an iron will that allows them to control their own emotions and appear to submit to the wishes of those around them, especially their husband. They are slow to anger, but erupt in a volcanic fury if pushed too far. Taurus women are extremely attracted to money, so their husbands must be good providers for them to be truly happy.

gemini As a Gemini man, you are restless and changeable, and these qualities often exasperate your wife and family. You are a sweet talker and can charm relatives who believe you to be extraordinary. You love to dress well, although sometimes quirkily, and you spend extravagant sums on clothes. A Gemini woman is an excellent hostess and has many friends who constantly fill her home. She can be a true soulmate when her spouse is in trouble, but if she feels betrayed by him, she will quietly exit from his life without causing too much distress to the family.

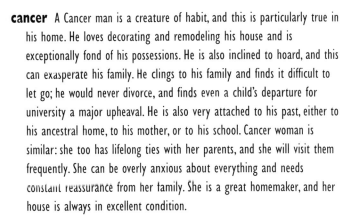

cancer A Cancer man is a creature of habit, and this is particularly true in his home. He loves decorating and remodeling his house and is exceptionally fond of his possessions. He is also inclined to hoard, and this can exasperate his family. He clings to his family and finds it difficult to let go; he would never divorce, and finds even a child's departure for university a major upheaval. He is also very attached to his past, either to his ancestral home, to his mother, or to his school. Cancer woman is similar: she too has lifelong ties with her parents, and she will visit them frequently. She can be overly anxious about everything and needs constant reassurance from her family. She is a great homemaker, and her house is always in excellent condition.

leo The mind of a Leo man is a marvelous encyclopedia of facts which his family love to listen to. If he learns patience, his children will put him on a pedestal for all his wit and intelligence. The one flaw he must strive to overcome is his an unsurpassed ego.

Unchecked, this leaves his family seething, and causes much backbiting and fury to be directed his way. Leo woman is happy only when she is pampered, and expresses her love to only a select few. She considers others to be privileged if they are allowed into her affections and guards her family like a lioness. She can be headstrong and argue relentlessly with her mate. However, if she feels he is worthy of respect, she will allow herself to be tamed and be an ideal partner.

virgo Men born under the sign of Virgo look for perfection in their loved ones, and even human flaws seem monumental to them. They must learn to accept people as they find them if they are to be happy at home. Virgos are slow to react to situations, but can make practical allies who stand by their family. A Virgo woman needs extra care and attention, as she is not easily pleased. However, she is one of the most committed women of the zodiac and will be solid in her support of the family.

libra These men look for honor and dignity before anything else and expect it of their families. A beautiful wife, a prestigious address, impeccably behaved children, these are things that are above money or fame. Libra woman is an expert at manipulating people to do whatever she wants, and the family will willingly dance to her tune. Her innate charm and apparent helplessness conceal an iron will. This is not to say that she is wicked, only that manipulation is second nature to her. She does this with such skill that it almost seems that it is the family looking after her, rather than the other way around.

scorpio This man does not give up easily on a relationship, and his sense of fairness ensures that a good deed or a kind word is amply rewarded. He has a strong sense of responsibility to the family, and his willpower guarantees that loved ones are always kept reasonably comfortable. He can also bring a religious or spiritual dimension into the home, but can become quite obsessive about this. However, he does not force his beliefs on others. Scorpio woman loves extremes. She can be maddeningly possessive or brutally aloof. She treasures her own space and occasionally needs some time away from her children. She is fiercely loyal, but her independent streak can make her appear too strong-willed to her relatives.

sagittarius Sagittarius man needs companionship but resents commitment. He is unlikely to be restricted to his home. Instead, he will wander around discovering new friendships and experiences. He loves his parents but values his independence more, and this sometimes makes him appear airy and aloof. Sagittarius woman is also difficult to capture and pin down. She loves adventure and brings a childlike enthusiasm into her home. Many Sagittarians have an unusual sense of fun and adventure and inhabit a world that they have created only for themselves.

capricorn This man's life is committed to achievement, and many Capricorns are willing to sacrifice their family life for it. They have a great desire to scale the heights of their chosen vocation, and their family relationships may suffer from neglect. He will, however, require a lot of attention, and an absent spouse may drive him into the arms of another woman. Capricorn woman is confident on the outside but very fearful within. She needs a strong man and a solid marriage to bring out the best in her. She will be attached to her mother throughout her life and will keep her family together in times of trouble.

Palmistry & the family

Refer to pages 56-61 for descriptions of the lines and mounts of the palm..

We can each understand aspects of our married life by reading the lines on our palm.

The line or lines of marriage are horizontal slashes just under the little finger on the outside edge of the palm. They lie between the line of heart—which runs along the top of the palm and underneath the fingers—and the little finger. These lines tell us not only about marriage but also about any strong love relationship that might not have culminated in a formal marriage but had a similar impact on our life. Only the long lines relate to marriage; the short ones denote deep attachments or near-marriages. Their position can also give a clue about the age at which the person may marry. The mounts of the hand—the raised portions of the palm—are also read in conjunction with the lines to form a complete picture.

When the longest line is close to the line of heart (running along the top of the palm beneath the fingers), there will be an early marriage, say in the early twenties. At the center of the space, the age for marriage will be in the mid to late twenties, specifically the age of twenty-eight. Three quarters upward, and marriage will occur between the ages of twenty-eight and thirty-five. Close to the little finger, and marriage will occur after the age of thirty-five.

An unbroken main line that is unmarked with crosses indicates that the marriage will be happy. If it curves down toward the line of Heart, it signifies that the person's spouse is likely to be the first to die. If the line curves upward, there is little chances of a marriage taking place at all.

If the main line is distinct but fine hairlines drop down toward the line of heart, the marriage will bear the strain of the spouse's health problems. If there is an island in the line, there will be trouble in the marriage, and a separation may occur.

When the main line divides at the end with a sloping fork dropping toward the center of the hand, there will probably be a divorce or legal separation.

A line full of islands and dropping lines denotes that the person should not marry, as no marriage will give happiness.

When the line of marriage sends a fine line to the Mount of Sun—which lies at the base of the ring finger—it signifies that the person will marry someone famous. When a deep line descends and intersects the line of marriage, there will be great opposition to the marriage.

When there is a line running parallel and almost touching the line of marriage, the person will have an affair or liaison after marriage.

The lines that tell us the number of children one is likely to have are fine upright lines from the end of the line of marriage. In some hands these lines are very faint and need to be observed with the help of a magnifying glass.

Generally broad lines denote males; finer lines denote females.

If the lines are straight and clear, the children will be strong and healthy. Wavy lines denote the opposite.

If one line is longer or more prominent than the others, it signifies that one child will be dearer to the parent than the others.

The numbers run from the outside of the marriage line toward the palm.

If a man's hand has prominent lines of children, he will be extraordinarily fond of children and will be a wonderful father.

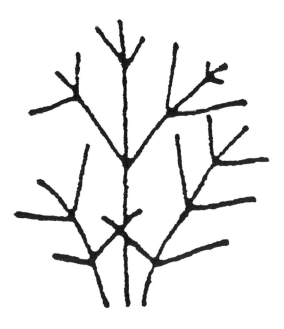

Love

A man necessarily gets what he deserves and is destined to get.
Garud Puran (c. A.D. 50)

India has never been shy of celebrating love and the erotic arts. Images
that are seen in art and architecture all over the country include
couples blissfully entwined in each other's arms, beautiful dancers in
revealing costumes, and courtesans adorning themselves to entice a lover.
These erotic images are in evidence even on temple walls and pillars,
where they were originally represented to symbolize the love of the
human soul for the Divine. Love and sex were considered almost spiritual
and were celebrated along with all the other arts.

There were special texts devoted to love and eroticism. The *Kamasutra* is
well known, and it details everything that makes sex a pleasurable and
uplifting experience. Another manual, the *Bhakti-Ratnakara* by Narahari
Chakravarti, lists 350 different types of love which include first love,
remembered love, wanton love, and desiring love.

It is little wonder, then, that lots of charms and luck tools were devised to
attract love luck into one's life. Women
wore lockets and amulets
containing an image of the
loved one in order to assure
fidelity. They also fasted (and
still do) on special days to
ensure success in love.
Some myths even
describe the
heroine etching
her lover's name
onto a tiny
seed and
planting it,
in the hope
that her love will
grow and flower.

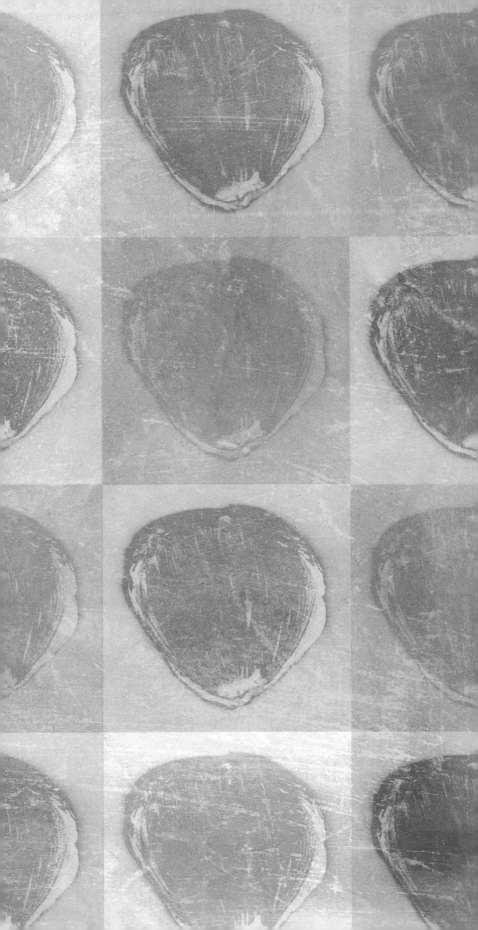

Gems & love

People the world over have believed that the special energies contained in gems can bring love and luck into their lives. Roman women wore amber to make their marriages strong and loving. The Greeks wore coral to avoid failure in love. In India, diamonds were worn to enhance sexual prowess.

red gems Wear a ruby if you wish to enchant your partner and keep him or her attracted to you. Rose quartz will help you focus your unconditional love and make you more appealing. All red gems ensure that your sex life is "hot" and "energetic".

orange gems Amber and other orange gems increase sexual potency and should definitely be worn if your body is less responsive than you would like it to be. In a romantic relationship, amber encourages you to be flexible and forgiving, so that any quarrels and tensions are quickly and smoothly resolved.

yellow gems If you are a somber person who is very conscious of what is construed as correct and incorrect behavior, wear a yellow gem such as topaz or citrine. These stones heal and nourish the nervous system and allow you to lighten up and have fun, which is an important prerequisite to finding and keeping love.

green gems The color of rejuvenation, green also signifies envy. Jealousy can stultify love and trust. If you are a possessive person who is constantly tempted to search through your partner's pockets and diary, or if you constantly nag your partner due to a burning suspicion in your own mind, then a green gem such as emerald, jade, tourmaline, or peridot is for you. These gems keep bitter feelings of jealousy under check and allow you to develop confidence in the honesty of your mate as well as in your own inner strength.

blue gems This is the color of idealism, and wearing a blue stone, such as sapphire, lapis lazuli, turquoise, or aquamarine, will make you seek out ideal love and friendship. These gems help love to be fulfilled and keep you aware of the positive energies of togetherness and compassion.

purple gems The color of healing is purple. A broken love relationship is always traumatic and can injure your spirit. When an affair ends, one almost feels unable to go on, but we all know that time is the best healer of all and that life continues. If you are in need of emotional pampering after a heartbreaking split, wear a purple gem such as amethyst, as this stone lessens pain and despondency.

white gems It is very difficult for many people to cope with the loss of sexual potency, and wearing a diamond will help alleviate the problem. Also, diamonds are known to move circumstances along, so if you find that your love relationship is in need of a boost, buy a diamond to wear. In India, pearls are worn by women who want to invite the luck of the Moon into their love life. The Moon, and therefore pearls, are symbolic of love and romance. Wear them to keep your love life peaceful but active.

Color & love

Love is a potpourri of emotions. We even experience love as a memory of touch, smell, taste, sound, or sight. A particular sight, a distinctive fragrance, a special taste, or piece of lilting music can all evoke happy memories of romance. In fact, few of us know that smells evoke colors, although we are attracted to fragrances that, in color therapy, possess pleasant colors. A large majority of people would say that rose, orange, vanilla, strawberry, sandalwood, lemon, and cinnamon smell wonderful. All of these have true, vibrant colors. Not everyone would agree that the smell of kerosene, fish, onions, eggs, garlic, or rubber is appealing, and sure enough, these odors generally have dull or cloudy colors. Lavender, pink, green, and light yellow are the most fragrant colors, whereas brown, black, and gray are low on the list of perfumes.

Our personalities in love are reflected in the colors that we choose to wear. Your partner may choose colors that are different from your own taste; but both of you should take care to complement each other. Often it is the colors belonging to your partner that are otherwise missing from your life; that is why you were attracted to him or her in the first place. For example, an introvert who prefers lavender may be enchanted by a gregarious person who is attracted to red and sparkles with wit and humor. On the other hand, an extremely unequal match may be detrimental to you, making you feel overwhelmed or restricted. A relationship needs a balance of energies to be successful.

What color person are you? In nature, each season has its own colour, feeling, and energy. We, too, are a part of this great natural rhythm which repeats itself in an infinitely repeating cycle. Our personal coloring also coincides with seasonal colors. We choose colors according to our seasonal type, and these not only reflect our personality but also help express our feelings naturally and completely.

the summer person You have the heat of the sun, the azure of the sky, and the energy of vast green and gold fields. Your skin tends to be translucent, pink, rose, or beige. Your hair is usually white, ash blond, gold, or mousy brown, and your eyes are hazel, blue gray, blue, or gray-brown. You have both masculine blue and feminine pink in your personality, which makes you both adventurous and sensitive. You find it difficult to express your true feelings and need to build your self-confidence in order to communicate your love to your partner.

the winter person Winter is a time of stark contrasts, darkness, and cold. It is reminiscent of white snow and dark nights. Winter people have distinctive coloring which makes them appear self-assured and in control. They generally have dark eyes, hair, and skin, ensuring that their eyes and teeth stand out in contrast. However, they may be diffident and shy away from the company of friends. Their emotions are strong, and although they seem uncommunicative, their love and loyalty will be deep.

the spring person Spring brings rejuvenating, pastel colors and the energy of new life and beginnings. Spring people have peachy, creamy skin, golden or dark-brown hair, and blue, green, or hazel eyes. They are full of vitality and have plenty of love to give, but their impulsiveness makes them flighty and superficial in their romantic relationships.

the autumn person Autumn is the season when leaves turn orange, red, and gold and fall to the earth in an eternal cycle of birth and death. Autumn people have similar coloring, with red, auburn, or strawberry blonde hair, golden to rosy skin, and golden, brown, or green eyes. In temperament, they are warm, rich, and full of depth and generosity. However, they are unpredictable and moody in love and dislike romantic routines that grow out of habit and familiarity.

139

These are the colors to wear if you want to attract love luck into your life:

red Wear red when you want to feel sensual and vibrant and when you wish to attract erotic love into your life.

pink Baby pink encourages an affectionate, gently caring relationship. Shocking pink speaks of seduction and passionate liaisons.

orange Wear orange when you want to enhance your *joie de vivre* or feel indulged in an existing relationship.

yellow This is the color of self-expression. Wear it if you need to reveal your feelings of love to someone but feel too tongue-tied.

green This is the color for you if you are obsessive in love and need to introduce a sense of balance to life. Wear green if you feel the need to give your partner breathing space.

blue Wear blue to promote quiet, peaceful love, especially when you feel the need for restful communication in between spells of frenzied romance.

purple Wear purple if you are anxious about the outcome of a love relationship. Purple helps you focus on higher energies and removes tension.

white Wear white only if you are overwhelmed by the demands of a lover and need a period of peace and quiet. White is the color of loneliness, so never wear it if you are feeling the pain of a broken love affair.

black This color will make you retreat into yourself, so avoid wearing it where your participation is essential. A new relationship needs communication and sharing, so try to highlight a black outfit with a touch of yellow or pink.

Symbols & love

Hindu symbolism is expressed in many forms, including architecture, dress, and furnishings. It is believed that particular symbols contain spiritual powers that will promote good luck. In India symbols of love luck decorate bedspreads, saris, and pillowcases, pillboxes or furniture in wood, and the pillars, ceilings, and walls of buildings. In Hindu mythology, coy maidens drew these symbols of love on fat, oval lotus leaves and sent them to their lovers as a secret message of longing. Of all the symbols of India, love symbols are the most celebrated in daily life:

bees In India, bees have always been associated with romantic and spiritual literature. The bowstring of Kamadeva, the god of love, is said to have been made of bees, and Goddess Parvati's lustrous black hair has been compared to a swarm of glossy bees. In Hindu philosophy, the human mind is compared to a bee, as both are flighty and easily distracted, and poets have compared the bee's thirst for nectar to the longing of the human soul for Divine love.

birds Indian music and dance celebrate the role played by birds in nurturing a romantic relationship. Parrots are messengers of love and are often depicted listening to a heroine's lovelorn sentiments and repeating them to the hero who is far away. Peacocks dance to the music of monsoon clouds and herald the season of love. The peacock feather is a symbol of the god Krishna, whose romantic exploits are legendary. The swan is the epitome of grace and beauty and stands for pure, selfless love. Birds are depicted in fabrics and *rangolis*, or floor patterns drawn in chalk, to bring good luck into one's home and life.

flame In Indian symbolism, the flame is representative of passionate but steadfast love. It is usually shown burning from an earthen lamp, or *diya*, frequently seen during the festival of Diwali.

flowers and creepers One of the earliest motifs used for luck was the *buta*, a stylized flower. Today this symbol of love is frequently used for embellishment. Exotic flowers are often grouped together to form stunning bouquets which are regal as well as glamorous. Flowers are bearers of the finer emotions of life. Love is captured in the softness of their petals, in the sweetness of the fragrance, and in the beauty of their color and shape.

The flower is often complemented by the creeper motif, which is a symbol of sensuality and beauty. It is sometimes depicted in rounded, freehand style or as a geometric form. There are several creeper motifs, each with a distinct name, such as *ashavalli* (creeper of hope) or *premlata* (creeper of love).

heart This symbolizes love the world over. Lovers send them in cards and on gifts, carve them into trees, and draw them on sandy beaches, declaring their love. Hearts encapsulate everything you feel and are an enduring sign of romance and allure.

the moon Hindus believe the Moon is a silent witness to nights of love and passion. It is reminiscent of clandestine meetings on scented terraces, of musical notes floating on the night breeze, and of lovers entwined in the fire of promise and mystery.

The moon is shown as full or as a crescent. It is beautifully depicted on a traditional black sari called the *chandrakala*. Embroidered in gold on a gauzy background of black, this sari is said to impart love luck to its wearer. Alternatively, wear a moon on a shawl or scarf, or hang one in your bedroom to remind you of romance and gentle sharing.

shells Since Vedic times, these have been valued as symbols of sensuality and passion. Hindu mythology describes the appearance of splendid shelled women and how the conch shell came into the world during the Churning of the Ocean. The conch, or *shankha*, is considered the most auspicious, and it is a popular motif on saris and in architecture. The conch also has a sexual significance because of the long opening and translucent, pink interior.

Metals & love

Indians believe that metals contain properties that influence our love luck. In West Bengal, in eastern India, married women wear a *loha*, or iron bangle, to bring love and longevity into their marriages. The most enduring token of love in India is gold. Its burnished lustre and incomparable value make it a worthy gift for lovers. Indian women are always loath to sell their gold, and would do so only in dire emergency.

Another love-attracting metal is silver. It is governed by the moon, who also rules over the home. Silver jewelery makes you more attentive to domestic matters and to the beauty of the home. It will make you look at love rationally and responsibly. It will also make you adventurous, and you will demand a certain degree of freedom for yourself.

If you tend to be selfish and uncharitable in love, try wearing a bracelet of copper. This metal represents the Sun, whose positive energy promotes generosity. It will also encourage fidelity, making your relationship strong.

Anyone who is restive and easily bored by relationships should keep an object made of lead close by, as this metal enables anchoring of the spirit. Alternatively, a love life fraught with arguments and quarrels can be improved through the use of brass objects. Gleaming and undented, these can bring harmony into your love life. Brass also prevents unreasonableness and intolerance. A brass vase, paperweight, or kitchen utensil should usher in lucky and loving times.

✳ Vastu shastra & love

Homes that are built in keeping with the principles of the ancient science of Vastu Shastra will invite good luck. Luck in a home encompasses love between the man and the woman who live inside its walls. Vastu Shastra emphasizes the bedroom, which is considered the temple of erotic love. The *Kamasutra*, the ancient Hindu treatise on sensuality, describes the decoration of a bedroom so that the experience of lovemaking is heightened. There are ways to decorate a bedroom that will drive away the shyness or hesitation of a coy maiden or increase the virility of a lover. Vastu Shastra describes the optimum direction for a bed and the ideal location for a bedroom, as well as the décor and uses of this room.

The guest bedroom should be in the northwest, but the main bedroom should be chosen carefully to enhance love luck:

north This direction ensures that the couple's life together will be full of financial tensions and mental unrest that will make a healthy, happy love life impossible.

northeast A bedroom that faces this direction will cause the couple to often become emotionally upset, with quarrels arising out of petty misunderstandings.

east The couple will suffer from constant ill health, and this will place a strain on their relationship.

southeast One of the partners will grow angry toward the other with alarming frequency. There may be bouts of sulking or even violent temper tantrums.

south This is a good direction for the main room, bringing happiness to the couple sleeping there.

southwest This is the best direction for the main bedroom. The couple will admire each other's good qualities, not concentrate on the other person's flaws.

west This is not a very good direction for the main bedroom, but children will flourish here.

northwest This bedroom will witness unhappiness and bickering within the relationship. There will be disagreement over who is the dominant partner, and love may become a distant memory.

The Vastu Shastra also describes the effects of sleeping with the head pointing toward a particular direction:

east The person will gain knowledge and be at peace in his or her relationship.

west The person will enjoy a fulfilling love life.

south The person will endeavor to create a warm and joyful partnership.

north The relationship will be full of tension, quarrels, and misunderstandings.

Decoration & uses of the bedroom

In India, the nuptial room is always a galaxy of color, fragrance, and beauty. Flowers such as marigolds and roses gently scent the air, and garlands of these blossoms are draped around the bed to create a special ambiance for the bridal couple. Flowers in the bedroom are always reminiscent of romance. According to Vastu Shastra, there should be pleasant paintings in the bedroom and never those of fighting beasts, war, or destruction. These negative images create unpleasant vibrations and encourage feelings of disharmony between the couple.

No dilapidated or unused goods should be stored in the bedroom, as this will cause cracks to appear in the relationship. The door of the bedroom should never be painted black or any dark color. This is because the door is symbolic of the mouth, and a black mouth encourages verbal disputes and arguments. In such a bedroom the couple's relationship will be stormy.

A faucet in the bedroom, or any water supply in the form of a basin or tank, will cause the woman to be suspicious of her partner.

The bedroom must be an intimate retreat for the couple alone. If friends are invited in to sit and chat, the woman of the house will become flirtatious and become attracted to another man.

The bedroom must always be well ventilated and naturally well lit. A dark room augurs bleakness in the relationship, whereas light makes it sparkle with joy.

The colors of the walls of the bedroom are also significant. Red denotes that the man will argue incessantly with his partner. Yellow indicates sensitivity, whereas blue shows that the couple consider material wealth to be more precious than their love for one another.

Numbers & love

The study of numerology provides early warnings about future problems or challenges so that we can prepare for them. The most important number that influences our love luck is our birth number. This is calculated by adding together the digits of the day on which you were born (for example, a person born on the twenty-seventh of a month will have the birth number nine). Your birth number reveals how you conduct your love life and the kind of lover you are:

number one This is the most powerful number in Indian numerology. Number one people adore their partner's flattery and bask in the glory of compliments and adulation. They are almost always given credit for their achievements. However, a lover may fail to keep promises made to them. They have excellent rapport with members of the opposite sex, and some will benefit from romantic liaisons with influential people. They can be rather dominating and are happiest when they are in command of the relationship. They also make ardent and faithful lovers. Number one people will bring harmony to their love life if they wear yellow, white, cream, and gold.

number two This is symbolically the number of the Moon. It contains the feminine counterpart of the Sun, which is number one, and therefore the pairing of a number one person and a number two person is almost always successful. Number two people believe in cooperation, as opposed to confrontation, and they are adept at handling misunderstandings in relationships. They are also very fond of socializing and parties and frequently add a vivacious zing to a relationship. If a number two person has a name or a spiritual number of five, there will be unhappiness in any love relationship that is embarked upon. Young women who are number two will find that wearing white, cream, or golden clothes will enhance love luck, and men who have a birth number of two should opt for light colors. Most number two people find a spiritual aspect in their love life and often marry around the age of thirty.

number three These people are cheerful, but require system and order in their lives. They are very selective in the choice of a partner, seeking someone who will be an asset to them. They also love to dictate terms and can be quite domineering. When married, they are entirely devoted to their spouse, but their bossy nature makes them prone to skirmishes within the relationship. Number three people's lucky colors are blue, lilac, mauve, purple, and violet; wear these for a fortunate love life.

number four These people are contrary. As a partner they can be quite irritating and might destroy an affair through their tendency to oppose everything that is said. They can also be very aggressive in matters of the heart and need careful handling if the relationship is to be successful. That said, they always settle down with accomplished partners who are loyal to them through thick and thin. Most number four people have a weakness for the opposite sex and treat each affair with as much intensity as the previous one. They should be cautious in their affairs of the heart; otherwise their behavior can jeopardize their progress and prosperity. Number four people often marry more than once or face separation within a relationship. Late marriages are also common. In their relationships, number four people give more affection than they receive. Their married life is often strained, although they make dependable, faithful partners. Number four people's lucky colors are electric blue, lightening gray, and all colors with shiny finishes.

number five This number seems to thrive on nervous energy and possesses a mercurial disposition—lively but inclined to change—like its ruling planet, Mercury. These people are sociable and live life to the full. They have magnetic personalities, but must be wary of misusing this quality while dealing with the opposite sex. Number five people tend to change partners frequently, but when married they enjoy a happy partnership. Number five people do face obstacles in their married life, and it is therefore imperative that they choose a partner whose birth number is in harmony with their own. This is usually another number five. Their prosperity is directly proportionate to the amount of support they receive from their spouse. The best colors for number fives are white, gray, yellow, green, and orange and they should opt for shades that glisten.

number six These people are blessed with a flexible nature which is affectionate and generous. They are ruled by the planet Venus and love beautiful things. They adore spending time with a partner in beautiful, natural surroundings. They dislike discord or quarrels and strive hard to maintain harmony in a relationship. They find themselves slavishly devoted to those they love, but they can be fairly obstinate as well. Number six people seem to find friendship with other people more easily than with their own family members, including their spouse. They love the company of the opposite sex and will pursue a prospective lover until they have achieved their aim. Their lucky colors are all shades of blue and pink, but they should stay away from black or deep purple.

number seven This number indicates a spiritual disposition and a tendency toward religious devotion. These people are fascinated by magic and the occult, and they tend to be sentimental in their relationships. They usually fall in love with a person whose birth number is six or eight. Their relationships are unstable, due to quick attachments and hasty actions. These people eventually turn to philosophy, and their partner may feel stranded and alone. Number seven people can be moody in matters of the heart. They are also heavily influenced by their families, which can put a strain on their relationship. In India, they are advised to opt for an arranged marriage, but throughout the world number seven people should be cautious in choosing a life partner. Lucky colors for number sevens are all shades of green, yellow, white, and all pale colors, and they should avoid dark colors.

number eight People with a birth number of eight face many hardships in their love life, as they are regularly misunderstood by their partner. They seem to lack the dexterity and finesse needed in delicate matters of the heart, and they often invest more love in a relationship that they receive in return. They are generally attracted to people who are practical and understanding and who share the same goals. They make good lovers and strive to learn the likes and dislikes of their partner. They pay attention to small details and make a partner feel cared for. However they are clear in their mind that any work that they undertake will always take precedence over their personal life. Number eight people should wear black, gray, white, purple, and blue.

number nine This number is ruled by the planet Mars, which controls fire and activity. It is also a symbol of the sex drive. Number nine people experience dramatic life changes through involvement with the opposite sex. These people will do almost anything to gain affection, and number nine men are heartbreakingly easy to manipulate. Number nine women are so fond of order that they are often attracted to men in uniform. The twenty-seventh year is often significant for number nine people, and many of them marry in this year. They must choose a partner who is devoted to them, or else life will become a living hell. They should not become involved with a person with a birth number of five or eight. Good colors for them to wear are pink, rose, crimson, and violet.

The first letter of your name

Your name alphabet, or the letter with which your name begins, reveals how you are likely to behave in a relationship. Its vibrations creates a powerful energy, which enhances certain traits and characteristics. Our names, by sheer repetition, give us the power to shape our destiny, and this inspires many people to alter their approach to romantic liaisons.

A Their love life begins early and they are good-natured and witty with people of the opposite sex. They should, however, check their impulsiveness.

B They are fairly shy and would rather follow than lead. They are submissive but crave perfection in everything.

C These people love change, but are also tempted to over-indulge in sex or in immoral pursuits. They often feel inferior and compensate for this with a series of romantic entanglements.

D They are generous and romantic. Although eager to treat their partner well, they need to keep petty jealousies at bay.

E These people look at everything from a sexual angle and enjoy speed, thrills and adventure. They are intense and wild in their relationships.

F They are fiery and passionate in love but shy away from being demonstrative in public. These people find it easy to be faithful to a partner.

157

G They are shy and undemonstrative in love, but deep within they have a core of sensuality. In spite of their reticence, love affairs seem to flood their lives.

H They live for today and never plan for tomorrow. They make caring lovers who offer to share responsibility for plans and actions.

I Their love life is cheerful and emotional. They prefer a direct approach and dislike playing emotional games. They should not allow their moodiness to hamper a love affair.

J They are outspoken but should be careful not to hurt their loved one's feelings. They smile a lot and create sunshine in their partner's life.

K These people make deliciously romantic partners, but they tend to over-indulge in sex. They must also resist a tendency to scrutinize their partner's behavior. In love, they are greatly influenced by a mother or a grandmother.

L They love being in love, but must be less egocentric if they are to find contentment. They are inclined to demonstrate their own superiority toward their partner, and this should be curbed.

M They are romantic and loyal but find it difficult to express their love. They seek true love constantly, but are more likely to find it in later life. Their love affairs are all meetings of heart and soul.

N These people have tremendous reserves of energy. They plan activities on a grand scale, but can become frustrated by the minor details, and they also need constant reassurance.

O Although these people have a wavering nature, they still try to be a good partner. They are fascinated by foreign cultures and often become involved with someone from another country.

P They love beauty and select good-looking partners. They are honest and loyal, and the decision to divorce will always follow an attempt to salvage the relationship.

Q Although these people's appearances are often magnetically appealing, many of them suffer from low self-esteem. As a result, they often have secret liaisons and extra-marital affairs.

R These people love those who possess the qualities in which they are lacking. They are passionate about love and look for soul mates who will accompany them through life's experiences.

S They usually take the lead in love affairs, although they would love to be surprised by a forthright partner. They are devoted to their loved one and can be shy with people of the opposite sex.

T They are romantic by nature, taking pleasure both in a loved one's achievements and in the good things in life. However, they can also be quite suspicious.

U These people endeavor to please their partners, sometimes at the cost of their own happiness. They are sympathetic to others, but can behave childishly in affairs of the heart.

V They are shy about approaching the opposite sex and very concerned about their public image. They dislike humiliating a partner in any way and are always supportive.

W They make enthusiastic lovers who believe in passion and sensuality. Although they often have secret relationships, these will not harm their primary relationship. They are not ill-intentioned and will avoid hurting their partner.

X They are reserved until they find a suitable partner. Thereafter, they shine at parties and events and enjoy attracting the attention of their lover. They are wary of feeling used and can be jealous in love.

Y These people have an ego that makes them the dominant partner in any relationship. They are cautious and slow in romance and have a streak of selfishness that is dangerous to a relationship.

Z They are sweet-tempered and get on fabulously well with the opposite sex. They also gain through such liaisons. Women are sometimes seen as over-liberal with their favors. On the whole they are domestic at heart.

Dreams & love

The most common dreams are about love, probably because it is the one thing we seek throughout our lives. We dream of our lovers or of being in love with someone else. We visualize objects that are associated with love and romance, but often we do not recognize the messages that they contain. By understanding the messages contained in our dreams we can influence our destiny. Here are a few love-related dreams:

balcony To see a balcony reveals that a sad separation from your lover will follow.

ballet This foretells quarrels or suspicion between lovers.

banana This denotes that you will be attracted to an unloving partner.

cushions To see pretty cushions denotes that you will be successful in love.

dew To see dew sparkling on grass means that you will soon be romantically involved with a rich person.

diving For lovers to dream of diving into a mirror-like pool indicates great happiness in love.

flute If a young woman sees herself playing a flute, she will fall in love, drawn by her sweetheart's magnetism.

fountain A fountain of cloudy water denotes being fooled by love.

frog If a woman sees a bullfrog, she will soon be attracted to a wealthy widower who already has children.

grass This is a very good omen and ensures the success of love after passing through troubled waters.

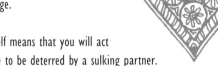

honey To dream of eating honey means that a love affair will lead to marriage.

knot To tie a knot yourself means that you will act independently and refuse to be deterred by a sulking partner.

kid goat This means that you will hurt a lover.

kiss To kiss you lover in the dark foretells danger and illicit relationships. If you kiss your sweetheart when it is light, your intentions are honorable. If your rival kisses your lover, you will temporarily fall from your lover's grace. If you see yourself kissing someone on the neck, you are seeking a passionate encounter. To see yourself kiss an enemy denotes that you will be reconciled with a disenchanted friend.

lips To see full, luscious lips means that your love will be reciprocated.

nettles If a young woman dreams of walking through nettles, she will soon be offered love by several men and be unsure which to choose.

nymphs To see nymphs frolicking in crystal water reveals that your dreams of love will come true. If a young woman sees herself as a nymph, it denotes that she will use her charms to manipulate or mislead men who are attracted to her.

paper If a young woman dreams of handling paper, she will soon be angry with her lover.

pearls If a woman dreams of receiving pearls from her lover, a wonderful relationship, free from petty jealousies and quarrels, awaits her.

raven If a young woman dreams of a raven, it is likely that a lover will betray her.

ruby To see a ruby foretells a successful love relationship, but to lose one indicates that your lover will not be charmed by your best qualities.

salt To see yourself eating salt denotes that your partner will leave you for someone younger.

strawberries If you see yourself eating glossy, crimson strawberries, your love will be reciprocated.

tunnel To see yourself going through a tunnel reveals that bad news will affect your relationship.

umbrella If you carry a leaky umbrella, your sweetheart will shortly cause you distress.

undressing If you see others undressing, some stolen pleasures will disturb your peace of mind. If you see yourself undressing, you will be the subject of hurtful gossip.

Astrology & love

It is probably true to say that the majority of people who read the astrology column in magazines do so to discover what their love life holds in store. If we understand our likely fate, revealed to us by our horoscope, we are able to chart a course to romance and to understand our lover's sometimes confusing behavior. Of course, bad behavior cannot be blamed entirely on astrology, and for any affair to flourish it must contain generosity of spirit.

aquarius The Aquarian man has a volatile mind which has no time for emotions. His indifference can be exasperating or confusing, but he is comfortable with that aspect of his character. He is forthright in love but seems to shield his innermost thoughts even from an intimate lover. He is willing to take his special lady into his world full of spice and passion, but there will also be forays into uncharted territory that she may not understand. The Aquarian woman needs tender loving care, but she is also a free spirit. She looks for intelligence and accomplishment and will do anything for a man who gives her integrity and friendship.

pisces This man has dual properties, just like his cousins Gemini, Sagittarius, and Virgo. While he is passionate about sensual pleasures, what he really desires is to be courted and wooed by a woman of quality. He is easily bored and needs constant emotional support. Pisces man weaves dreams that look irresistible, but his star sign, of two fish swimming in opposite directions, denotes the state of his emotions. He is loving and generous but unsophisticated in the art of romance. Pisces woman is truly feminine and her allure lies in her helpless and delicate persona. She is idealistic when choosing a mate, and her yardstick may be the hottest young movie star. She needs a great deal of practical wisdom in a man for him to be a truly ideal companion.

aries This man loves to be first in a woman's life and likes to believe that there has been no other man before him. He is also looking for a partner who will gently push him toward success without pressurizing him. In return, he will be affectionate and sentimental toward his partner. She will, however, need to remove his rose-tinted glasses from time to time without allowing him to become disillusioned. The Aries lady loves to be complimented on her efficiency. Her man must be powerful but should also allow her spirit some adventure. She is looking for a mate who will love her for her practical mind and can look beyond her feminine charms, as feminine games hold no amusement for her. She will support her ideal mate forever.

taurus This man is so fond of socializing he can seem compulsively flirtatious. His ideal mate is elegant in the way she dresses, converses, and conducts herself. She will also let him wander a bit and ignore his perpetually twinkling eye. Taurian woman looks for a mate who can give her the good things in life. He must be rich, and in return she will forsake all social events, charities, and friends to make her man's life a bed of roses. The best dinners, a beautifully groomed partner, and a steamy sex life await the man who captures her heart.

gemini This man loves whichever woman he is currently with and can fabricate quite a story to conceal his other liaisons. He can create instant excitement in a relationship, but his moods can also spiral down, submerging the relationship in his deep depression. He demands his partner's time and attention constantly and can become sulky if she is preoccupied. When he is not fascinated by the female world around him, he can be an ardent and devoted lover. Gemini woman looks for a sweetheart who will love her in spite of her restlessness and changeability. She creates a whirl of activity around herself and likes her mate to join in. This woman is not the ideal partner for a jealous or possessive man!

cancer This man is touchingly sensitive and will hold on to the memory of a love affair long after it is over. He will never hurt his partner or risk losing her trust but he will want her to settle into his ways without making too many changes. He dislikes new routines or new pastimes and can be bad tempered or nervous around someone who is looking for new excitement every day. Cancer woman is frantic about finding Mr. Right. She sees an affair as a means to marriage. She looks for someone who can look after her, but she can be quite difficult to please. Her imagined woes can mar a good relationship, and her man will often have to smooth her ruffled feathers by sweet talking and laying her fears to rest.

leo If you pursue an affair with this man, he will have to be your Sun, Moon, and stars. He will rule your life, tell you what to wear and how to eat, but he will also infuse your life with glamour and exotic beauty. Leo man looks for perfection in a mate and appreciates long hours spent in the beauty salon. He makes his sweetheart feel special, as long as she is not stealing his limelight. Leo woman has to be equal to her man and will never allow

herself to be dominated. She has a challenging air about her that men find irresistible, but her icy comments can quickly deter unsuitable partners. She makes a loyal companion to the man she considers to be her ideal mate.

virgo Think of total self-sacrifice in a love affair and you will see Virgo man. Although he is slow to take action even when he has fallen in love, he is a thoughtful lover who prizes beauty and efficiency over pure feminine wiles. He will not be overly romantic, bringing flowers and gifts, but he will share even the most boring chores. Virgo woman looks for perfection. Repelled by clumsiness or a scruffy appearance, she makes a wonderful mate for someone who is ambitious and will endeavor to live up to her expectations.

libra The Libran man is the quintessential charmer. He loves beautiful women and will flirt both subtly and outrageously. He holds honor dearest to his heart, and will be faithful in a relationship that he finds perfect. Libran woman is made of steel, but her attraction is her apparent helplessness and dependency on her man. Of all the signs, she is the most manipulative, subtly achieving exactly what she desires.

scorpio This man is obsessive in love. When he falls in love with a woman, she becomes the sole object of his devotion, and he will do crazily passionate things to win her affection. However, the male Scorpio male also feels a powerful need to control his partner, and if upset by her, he will slide into discontentment. Scorpio woman will hypnotize her man with her magic eyes and passionate, zestful nature. She gives and expects complete fidelity and will be the woman her partner fantasizes about all his life. Her love life is ruled by sex, and she is the perfect example of fire in the bedroom and ice in the living room.

sagittarius This man is so generous with his attentions that his woman hardly listens when he explains that all he wants is her friendship. He will seem to woo her but will move on to his next venture, leaving her behind.

He hates ultimatums and restrictions and will love a woman for her companionship and trust. Never ask him outright for a commitment, or he may be scared off. Sagittarius woman is the eternal do-gooder, sacrificing the best things in life for what she believes is her real calling, standing by her mate. She can be hasty in love and will have several affairs.

capricorn This man loves his woman while he is with her but will not daydream about her when they are apart. Although he is generally devoted, he is capable of being unfaithful. His life is ruled by achievement and money, but a rich Capricorn man can also sweep a woman off her feet with passion and romance. Conversely, a Capricorn man who is still struggling in his career can sink into depression, taking his partner with him. Capricorn woman appears to be totally in command of her emotions, but she is forever questioning her own choices in love. This indecision makes her extremely appealing to men, but she looks for devotion and persistence in her ideal mate.

Palmistry & love

Love plays almost a central role in the theatre of life, and the lines of the hand bear testimony to this. The line that runs along the top of the palm under the fingers is the line of heart, or the mensal. There are several mounts—raised portions of the palm—between the fingers and the line of the heart: the mount of Jupiter at the base of the index finger, the mount of Saturn under the middle finger, the mount of the Sun under the ring finger, and the mount of Mercury at the base of the little finger. The line of the heart should be clear, deep, and evenly colored. This is the line that tells our love story, including the romantic inclinations that we carry in our psyche.

When the line of the heart rises from the center of the mount of Jupiter, it denotes a supreme kind of love. The person considers love to be worship and is strong and considerate in a relationship. Such a line makes the person seek a mate of the same or higher social standing and expect their lover to be noble in love. Needless to say, this person does not indulge in affairs lightly.

167

If the line touches the first finger itself, the person enters love relationships blindly, idolizing the object of their affection. They see no faults in their partner, and when the truth finally becomes apparent, they are often inconsolable. Their distress is largely due to their own loss of face rather than the imperfections of their mate.

When the line arises between the first and second finger, the person is even tempered and full of feeling in matters of the heart. Their passions have the nobility of the Mount of Jupiter and the ardor of the Mount of Saturn, between which this line lies.

A line that arises out of the mount of Saturn indicates an individual whose affairs are passionate but rather selfish in nature. His or her selfishness and sensuality are even more pronounced if the line actually touches the middle finger.

If the line of heart sweeps right across the palm from one side to the other, this indicates possessive love which leads to devastating jealousy and friction in relationships.

When the line is crisscrossed with countless fine lines, the person will be fickle and flirtatious and will find it difficult to maintain a lasting relationship.

A broad, chained line that arises out of Saturn indicates contempt for the opposite sex. A broad line that is pale in color denotes indifference, whereas one that is bright red shows violence in passion.

If the line of heart appears low on the palm, almost close to the line of head, the heart will always win over the head.

However, if the line of heart is high on the palm and the line of head creeps up toward it, the head will rule the heart, making the person appear cold and calculating.

If the line is broken, there will be failures in love, as follows: if it is broken under the mount of Saturn, love will end through accident and fatality; if it is broken under the mount of Sun, love will fail through pride; if it is broken under the mount Mercury, love will fail through folly and immaturity.

If the line has a small fork on the mount of Jupiter—at the base of the index finger—the person has a true, straightforward nature which is capable of honest and devoted love.

When the line of heart curves upward toward the base of the fingers, it describes a person with a happy nature who enjoys falling in love. If it dips down toward the line of head, it denotes broken love affairs early in life.

If the line forks with one branch on the mount of Jupiter—at the base of the index finger—and the other between the first and second fingers, it signifies joyful liaisons. If the second branch rests on Saturn—at the base of the middle finger—it indicates a tendency to be erratic in one's affections, blowing hot and cold until one's partner is thoroughly exasperated.

When this line is thin and devoid of any branches, the person is cold and ungiving in matters of the heart. If this thin line moves toward the side of the hand, it indicates possible sterility.

When the line of heart, head, and life are all joined, the person can be extremely selfish in attaining his or her desires.

Someone who has no line of heart, or only a superficial one, will never fall deeply in love but can be sensual if the hand is soft. A hard hand accentuates cold-heartedness.

If a line of heart exists but fades away, it denotes that the person has been so terribly disappointed in love that he or she has become irrevocably cold and indifferent.

The girdle of Venus is another line on the hand that indicates the romantic life of the individual. This is an arc that curves from between the first and second finger to the third and fourth finger. Its existence denotes a person who is difficult to please in love, someone who is demanding and exacting and who can never be happy. Its absence is a far luckier omen.

Money

Distribution of accumulated wealth
Provides the safety measure,
Just as ebb and flow
Preserve the pool of water.

Chanakya's *Neeti Shastra* (between 350 and 275 B.C.)

In India the use of coined money began around 500 B.C., but riches have been coveted and treasured since the beginning of time. People the world over dream of becoming fabulously rich overnight, and it is fair to say that, in many ways, money makes the world go around.

Although we like to think that the world has become materialistic in recent times, for thousands of years people have used a variety of devices to enhance their wealth. The worship of Lakshmi, the goddess of good fortune and wealth, began in India more than 3,000 years ago. Lakshmi is depicted as a beautiful woman in a flowing sari, standing inside an open pink lotus flower and showering gold coins on her devotees. Each year, during the festival of Diwali, there is a special day dedicated to the worship of this goddess. The doors of homes and offices are left ajar throughout the evening, so that she can symbolically enter. Her image is decorated with fresh, fragrant flowers, and there is much feasting in her honor. Because of the transient nature of money, she is also called Chanchala, or fickle.

In this chapter, we look at how we can increase our luck by using each of the luck tools when earning an income through employment, investment, or an inheritance.

Gems & money

In ancient India, kings and emperors were advised by sages to wear certain gems in order to increase their wealth and empire. This belief holds true even today, when countless Indians wear specific gems to increase their fortunes.

Indians are great believers in the clarity of gemstones. According to Indian gemology, there are certain malefic marks within gemstones that can influence their effectivity. In the case of bright stones such as diamonds, a *bindu*, or a dark spot, can dramatically diminish the wearer's wealth and property. Crow's foot cracks emanating from a single point can gradually dissipate all riches, and a crack in the stone is considered so inauspicious that it can transform a king into a pauper. In the case of dark stones, such as the ruby, a drop-shaped inclusion will destroy the wearer's home and wealth, and a discolored stone will drain money away like water. The following gems have specific money-luck properties:

red gems As well as instant success, rubies can bring wealth into the home more quickly than expected. Rubies are especially successful in property or money matters that involve government or legal procedures.

Wear rubies set in gold on the index or ring finger. You should start wearing your ring on a Sunday. Another dark red gem, called hessonite, helps maintain wealth and protects the wearer from sudden misfortune.

yellow gems   One of the most popular gems in India is the yellow sapphire. It can be seen sparkling on the index finger of many a businessman and entrepreneur. The best yellow sapphires come from Sri Lanka. The sapphire must be set only in gold and worn for the first time on a Thursday after being properly energized— a cleansing ritual in which it is submerged in milk—for it to be truly effective. Yellow sapphire enhances and maintains one's financial status. The wearer can become rich through honorable means. Another yellow gem favored by people who want immediate riches is cat's eye. This stone brings fortunes to those who gamble at horse racing, in casinos, or in lotteries and to those who speculate in stocks and shares.

green gems   The wearer of a green gem, such as an emerald, will find that his or her drive to earn more money is enhanced. This stone encourages ambition and a cautious approach when assessing a situation before making an investment. Emeralds should be set in gold and worn on the little finger.

blue gems   Sapphire is considered the most magical stone of all. However, it can also cause fluctuations in the wearer's fortune, so it is important to test one by wearing it for a few days. Sapphire can restore lost wealth and property and significantly improve the financial status of the wearer. A blue sapphire should be set in a white-colored metal, such as platinum or steel, and worn on the middle finger.

white gems A diamond can take its wearer to the pinnacle of success. It favors a temperament that enjoys wealth and luxury. Diamonds should be set in gold and worn on the little finger. Pearls, although not technically gems, are still included in this category because of their rarity and value. Pearls and moonstones both help to clarify the mind before one makes a judicious investment. They should be set in silver or platinum and are best worn on the little finger.

Color & money

Indian people believe that colors have distinct vibrational fields and that each color can interact with a receptive personality, inviting good fortune. Color therapy is, however, almost entirely dependent upon our emotions. Therefore wearing or keeping a particular color close by will not necessarily invite a material attribute such as money into your life. However, the color yellow, for example, will help sharpen your faculties when making decisions about money. This color promotes clarity of thought and the ability to make informed decisions.

purple The color purple has historically been associated with royalty and riches, perhaps because in days gone by the dye was so expensive that only the very rich could afford it. Believers in color therapy wear purple to boost their financial luck and overall prosperity.

white If you feel the need for self-discipline, wearing white will help you exercise thrift and caution.

green Green is the color of prosperity and plenty, giving a boost to moneymaking schemes and ideas. It is also the color of youth and energy, so wear green to stimulate action and adaptability.

red Red is for those involved in risky, daredevil professions in which financial decisions involve a degree of uncertainty. This color helps ensure the success of plans that appear too adventurous.

blue Blue, especially pale blue, is the color of generosity and lavish spending. This is the color to avoid if you are in a financial tight spot. Wear dark blue when making investments, as it seems to convey financial stability and good judgment.

black People who wear black are highly respected and well able to handle family funds.

gray Gray instills hard work, perfectionism, and respect for rules, and those who wear it may sacrifice personal gain for the good of the community.

In addition to the intrinsic properties of color, Indians believe that our personalities fall into one of five categories: fire, earth, air, water, or space. Each personality type is attracted to colors that emphasize its characteristics and repelled by colors that depress its spirits. Therefore, a fire person may find red energetic and green hopelessly dull, whereas an earth person is attracted to browns and greens but does not appreciate blue.

Symbols & money

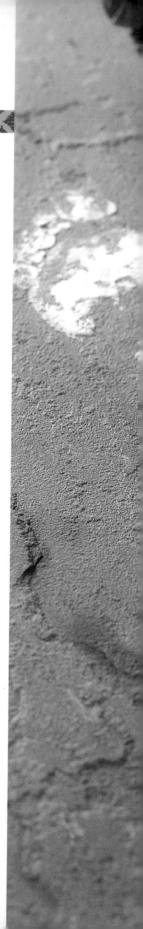

The Bombay Stock Exchange is as noisy and apparently chaotic as any other around the world. There are wild gestures, frenzied phone calls, and shouting matches over people's heads. However, there is possibly one difference: several of the dealers have specific luck symbols in evidence on their desks or tucked away in a wallet or purse. These symbols are lovingly placed with the complete faith that they will help bring the fabled windfall that will make them millionaires in an instant.

Lakshmi's footprints If you look closely at a traditional Hindu doorway, treasury cupboard, or money chest, in all likelihood you will see a set of tiny, stylized footprints. These are an ancient graphic symbol of Lakshmi, the goddess of wealth and luster. It is believed that the goddess brings great fortunes and financial luck.

The footprints are drawn with powder on the floor as a *rangoli* or stamped onto doors and walls. An interesting part of the Hindu wedding is the new bride's entrance into the matrimonial home. She is considered the Lakshmi of the house and is asked to step into a tray of wet color. She then walks into the home, leaving auspicious prints representative of the goddess. This signifies that she, too, is the harbinger of prosperity and plenty.

elephant This animal is loved by all Indians. It was a source of curiosity to the Aryans, who came to India in the first millennium B.C. In the Sanskrit text the *Rigveda*, the elephant was described as th "animal with a hand," due to its strange trunk. The elephant is extremely significant in Hindu mythology. In early lore, all elephants were white, had wings, and were compared to snowy clouds. In time they lost their wings, but to this day, they continue to be symbolically cloudlike. In fact, they are compared to a monsoon cloud, which brings rain and prosperity and is therefore considered very auspicious.

Elephants are symbols of wealth and riches and are represented on embroidered or woven fabrics, as well as on furniture. In medieval India, people believed that anyone who owned an elephant must be very affluent, and as a result its representation as a bearer of wealth progressively strengthened. Until very recently, only the maharajas of royal India could maintain a procession of elephants, which would be adorned in richly ornamental coverings and led out on ceremonial occasions.

godlings According to Hindu mythology, the guardian of the world's gold, silver, gems, and other treasures is Kubera. He is helped by several godlings called *yakshas* and *kinnaras*. These minor deities are depicted as beautiful beings, sometimes with heads or bodies of beasts and birds, such as the horse or the eagle. They are considered to be sylvan spirits because they know of treasures buried in the mountains or in the roots of mighty trees. Treasure chests and cabinets are often embellished with these creatures for protection.

wheel A continuous circle capable of perpetual movement, the wheel is a potent symbol of energy. It signifies the constant flow of wealth and is often drawn on the doors of houses, inviting good fortune inside. The direction in which it moves is extremely important—wheels must rotate

in a clockwise direction to be fruitful, whereas wheels that move in the opposite direction are associated with evil and sorcery.

cow The cow holds pride of place among all the animals of India. It is considered divine and is worshiped all over India as the bestower of prosperity. In *Rig-veda*, the cow is described as "not-slayable," as she represents wealth and good fortune. In a pastoral society, such as India was and largely remains, herds of cows were an important marker of wealth, and all the products of a cow (milk, dung, urine) were used in different ways. The cow is still symbolic of wealth and believed to enhance one's riches through honorable means. One of the best-loved cows of Hindu mythology is Kamadhenu (wish-cow), who was born out of the Great Churning of the Ocean. She is believed to be a magical cow of plenty who can make all of her owner's dreams come true. Hindus believe in the efficacy of the cow so strongly that many start each day by feeding a little grass to a cow before setting off for work. Owners of cows have made a mini-business of this, and even city streets have a cow and a bundle of grass at each corner.

snakes In Hindu mythology, great snakes are the custodians of the glittering treasures hidden under land and sea. They are believed to use their wisdom and magic to guard those riches. Special snakes are said to have gems unsurpassed in beauty and brilliance embedded in their hoods. Snakes are used to decorate those places where wealth is stored, ensuring its safety.

Snake worship is common in India. Temples are dedicated to snakes, and special festivals are held in their honor.

Metals & money

In India, gold and silver are the metals of prosperity. Women are actively encouraged to wear gold to proclaim to the world that the home from which they come is financially stable. They are also expected to wear gold because it is believed to attract more wealth into the home. When people buy a plot of land to construct a home or an office, it is traditional to bury a tiny gold coin in the foundations so that prosperity will always reside in the building. Fine gold foil or wires are also embedded in the walls. It is considered fortunate to use silverware in the home because this represents an invitation for wealth to enter. Newborn babies are always given presents of silver to wish them a life of prosperity and plenty. In fact, silver is so closely associated with opulence that the choicest candies are wrapped in an edible silver foil called *varq*. This is also seen on sumptuous meat dishes served at lavish banquets.

Indians' love of metals and their respect for its symbolic evocation of wealth are evident in the wide array of handcrafted objects sold throughout the country. Delicate filigree screens in silver, latticed iron windows, decorative copper plates and relief-work urns or trays can be found in many Indian homes. Each part of the country specializes in a unique form of metalware, used to invite luck into local homes. South India produces exquisite bronze statues with finely etched faces and sinuous bodies. From the west come tinkling bells and more expensive silver swings which beckon you to rest on a hot afternoon. North India is famous for its brassware, and the east is ashimmer with the sparkle of brassware and fine silver jewelery.

Vastu shastra & money

The ancient science of Vastu Shastra depends largely upon astrology and the eight compass points. For example, the north is ruled by Kubera, the god of wealth, and according to Vastu Shastra this is the ideal direction for the storage of wealth. Money, jewelery, and any cabinets holding valuable possessions should be placed in the northern part of the house, near the southern or western wall so that they face the east or north and attract greater wealth.

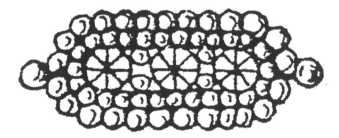

Many of a building's features can affect the flow of money into a house. One is the existence of a large, open space directly in front of the house. Such spaces are governed by the malefic planet Rahu (found only in Hindu astrology), which suppresses growth and prosperity. Another factor is the nearby presence of a road's end—that is, if the home is located at a T-junction. Governed by Rahu, road ends will cause the family's wealth to run dry.

There should never be thorny plants or heaps of stones and rubble in front of a house, as this indicates that any income made by the family will be the result of great hardship and adversity. The income will also be insufficient and will cause tension within the home. Similarly, a laundry or hairdresser directly opposite the house will ensure that money comes into the home only occasionally.

If there is a dilapidated or unused house directly opposite your own, you will discover that your expenses always exceed your income and that you constantly owe money to creditors. A lake across the road from your home will have a similar effect. However, such problematic areas in front of the house can be corrected by planting beautiful flowering shrubs or, better still, the holy basil (*Tulsi*) plant, which is considered auspicious all over India and grows well during the summer all over the world.

One should also ensure that all steps leading up to the house are free of cracks. Broken stairs are a sure sign that the inhabitants will face financial calamity. Repair chipped stairs and tiles as soon as you spot them. The main door should be beautiful, without cracks or blemishes. If possible, auspicious money-luck symbols, such as an elephant, flowers, or an image of Lakshmi, should be used to decorate the door.

If you face a wall when entering your main door, this signifies that all prosperity coming into the house will be obstructed and that income will arrive in short bursts. It also signifies that any wealth coming into the house cannot be enjoyed immediately. In this case, auspicious symbols should be suspended on the wall to invite good luck inside.

The main door frame should ideally be larger than the remainder of the doors in the house. This is because, symbolically, any good fortune that enters should not be allowed to escape easily through the other doors. It is inadvisable to leave an apartment vacant for a long period of time, but if this cannot be avoided, light a lamp in order to prevent money-luck from withering away. These days, it is easy enough to use a timer switch, so that a light can remain on during the evening.

Numbers & money

You can use numerology to ascertain the influence of numbers on your wealth. Your birth number reveals your attitude toward money and how it will come to you. Calculate your birth number by adding together the digits of the day you were born (for example, a person born on the twenty-seventh of a month will have a birth number of nine).

number one This is a very fortunate number which attracts wealth and power. These people usually benefit from an inheritance bestowed by their father. Their financial fortunes grow steadily over the years, but number one people remain thrifty. Parental property, too, comes their way, and they make profits through real estate. Their lucky days for all financial decisions and dealings are Sunday and Monday.

number two This person is not a quick decision maker and does well as a business associate of a forceful partner. Number two people tend to obtain money spasmodically, and even legacies come as a windfall. They often benefit through commissions and indirect dealings. Their lucky days in fiscal matters are Sunday and Monday.

number three These people rise in their financial status by degrees and rarely descend from that position once reached. However, they are quite extravagant with money. Their wealth usually arrives after their forty-fifth year. Their lucky days are Tuesday, Thursday, and Friday.

number four These people are rarely as successful as others in material pursuits, and they are unaffected by the spectacle of others competing for wealth. If they inherit or receive money, how they use their fortune is a source of great surprises for everyone around them. They are favored with gains from property and inheritance, and their assets start to build from their thirtieth year. However, their finances fluctuate considerably, and they would do well to refrain from gambling and speculation. Their lucky days are Saturday, Sunday, and Monday.

number five These people dislike mundane routines and often find themselves in situations where they can make money quickly. They have a flair for making money through novel ideas and approaches, and they are speculative in their investments. They keenly observe the stock markets and are willing to take risks when they expect a sure profit. Their lucky days are Wednesday and Friday.

number six These people love to spend their money on the arts and the finer things in life. They would forsake wealth for personal honor and reputation but can be lavish spenders. They usually start making a good amount of money from their forty-second year onwards. Their lucky days are Tuesday, Thursday, and Friday.

number seven Although they cannot be called materialistic, number seven people make money through ingenuity and hard work. They often make donations to charities or to less fortunate relatives and friends. They should never speculate or gamble. Lucky days for number sevens are Sunday and Monday.

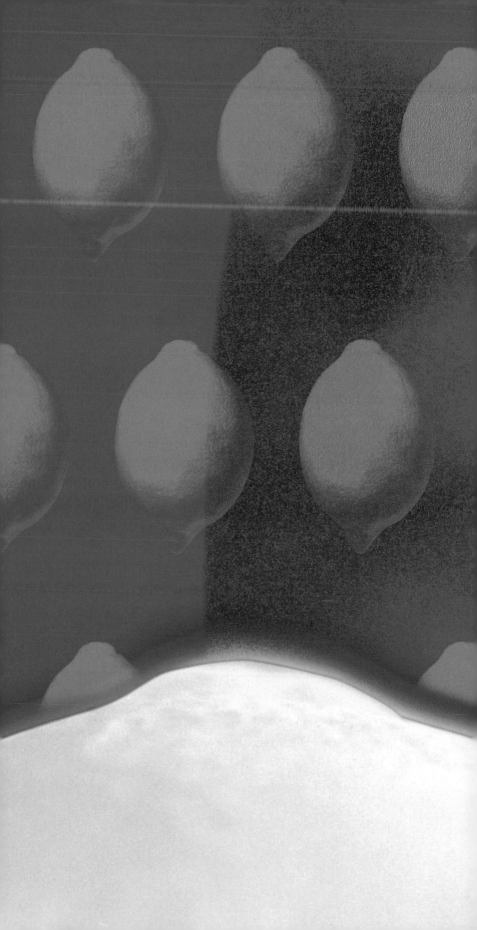

number eight These people are either very successful or wallow in the depths of failure. This is not a very fortunate number to be born under, as an individual has to face great upheavals if he or she is to become financially secure. Lucky days are Saturday, Sunday, and Monday.

number nine This number can be financially successful if decisions relating to money are made on Tuesday. Thursday and Friday are also fairly lucky days. It is advisable to take action on days of their own birth number, that is, on the ninth, eighteenth, or twenty-seventh of any month.

The name number is also frequently used to seek luck in money matters. This is the sum of the number values of the letters in your first and last names (see page 40 and opposite). A birth number is reduced to a single digit, but its prior value is also significant. While the numbers one through nine are considered material numbers, those from eleven onward are known as compound numbers and relate to the spiritual aspects of life, in particular our feelings of self-worth. The following are especially lucky for financial success:

number fourteen This is a fortunate number for money and speculation, but always remain cautious about the foolish mistakes or advice given by others.

number fifteen This number helps you obtain money from others as an inheritance or through business.

numbers twenty-three and twenty-four Both of these are fortunate numbers which help you realize your financial plans.

number twenty-seven This numbers helps you earn fiscal returns from your intellectual or creative pursuits.

number thirty This number will encourage you to forsake material wealth in favor of spirituality. It can be spiritually powerful; a materialistic person should use it cautiously.

How to make numbers work for you

Numerologists maintain that it is essential that your birth and name numbers (calculated using your first surname) be in harmony. In India, followers of numerology will often change the spelling of their given name to match the sum of their birth number. My birth number is calculated as follows:

M O N I S H A   B H A R A D W A J

4 + 7 + 5 + 1 + 3 + 5 + 1   2 + 5 + 1 + 2 + 1 + 4 + 6 + 1 + 1

= 26   = 23

8   5 = 13 = 4

If had a birth number of five I would need to add one more to my name number for both vibrations to harmonize. Therefore, I might add an A to the end of my first name, making it Monishaa. This would give me a total of

27 = 9   for my first name

23 = 5   for my surname

14 = 5   which is in harmony with my birth number and therefore sure to bring me luck!

Dreams & money

Dreams are mirrors that reflect our subconscious selves. If we analyze our dreams, we can decipher our deep-rooted attitudes to money, poverty, and wealth, including our notion of relative comfort and good fortune. For example, one person may view ownership of a mansion and three luxury cars as the ultimate mark of success, whereas someone else may be satisfied with a comfortable home and a car that runs. By revealing our most powerful needs and attitudes, dreams provide the self-knowledge we all need in order to prosper.

coins Gold coins are messengers of prosperity; silver coins foretell troubles; and copper ones symbolize physical difficulties.

gold If you see yourself receiving gold, money will soon follow. If you are a woman and you see yourself receiving jewelery, you may soon marry a wealthy but materialistic man. If you lose gold, one of your most remarkable opportunities will slip through your hands.

inheritance If you see yourself receiving an inheritance, you will soon accomplish your goals.

jewelery If this is broken, there will be a delay in achieving your goals, whereas sparkling jewelery is a good sign. If you inherit jewels, you will gain through unconventional means, which may not leave you completely satisfied. To see yourself wearing jewelery is an excellent omen.

money If you find money, your little problems will disappear and you will soon be happier. If you save money, it is a good financial omen. If you give money to someone, there will be a mishap. To see yourself stealing money shows that you are in some kind of danger.

peacocks This denotes that there will be a constant waxing and waning of riches in your life. Furthermore, you may become fabulously rich, but all fortune will be overcast by the shadow of sorrow.

riches This is a good sign and shows that you will gain wealth through hard work and industry.

silver This is a warning that you are dangerously close to looking at material wealth as a source of true happiness. If you find a silver coin, you are judgmental of others and hasty in your decisions. To see silverware denotes that you are dissatisfied with an ongoing project.

yellow To see yellow clothes denotes that you will soon be more secure financially. If you see the yellow clothes in glimpses or in fading light, it denotes the reverse.

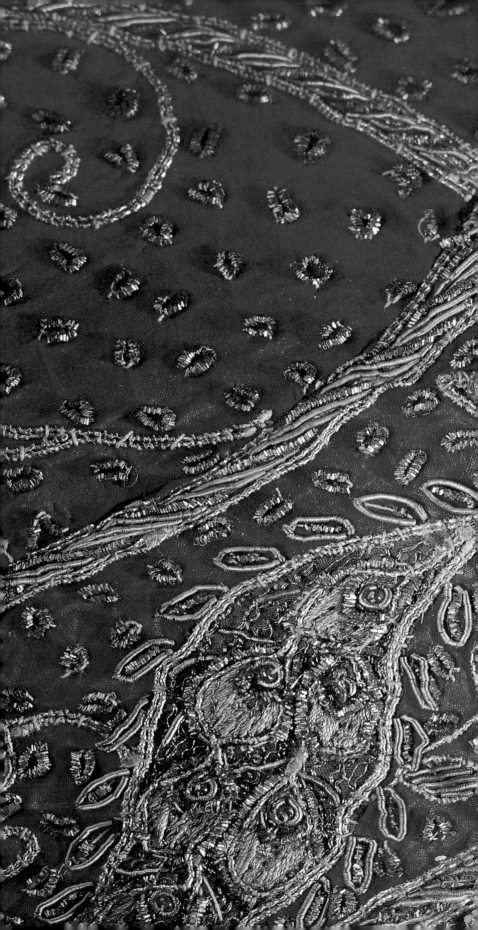

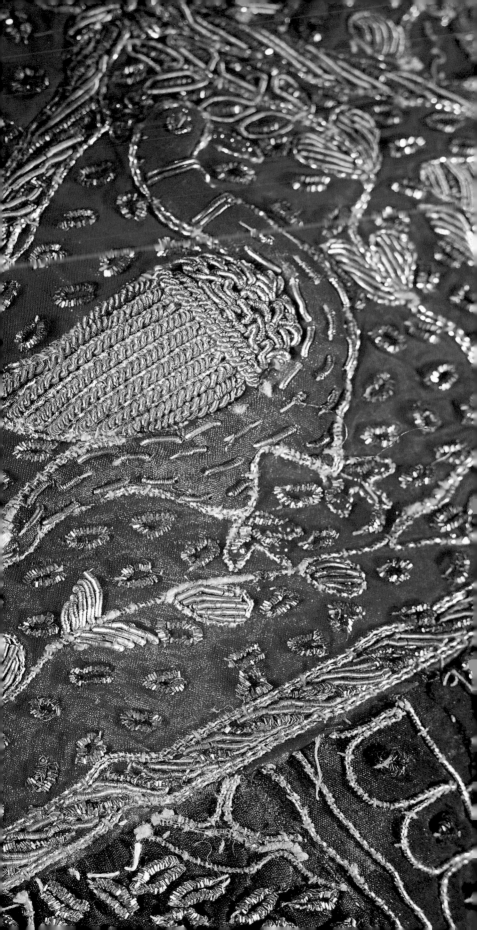

Astrology & money

When a person is born, the planetary bodies occupy definite points in the sky. Their positions are recorded in a birth horoscope, which is divided into twelve houses. The second, ninth, and eleventh houses of a horoscope govern financial matters. In Indian astrology, the planet Jupiter is the ruler of wealth, and if at the time of birth Jupiter lies in any of these houses, great wealth is foretold. A person's finances will be stable if Venus and Mars occupy two of these houses, whereas Saturn's presence is unfavorable. The fourth house represents immovable property and luxury, and the presence of Venus here foretells many comforts.

Astrology provides clues for enhancing luck, but you must believe you can make a difference. There are no guarantees that life will dramatically change for the better, but luck tools can provide guidelines to what may or may not work. They can also suggest ways of dealing with aspects of your life you cannot change, so that you fully enjoy your quota of happiness and success. While the secrets of a birth horoscope can be revealed only by a competent astrologer, people also display certain characteristics depending on the month in which they were born. Understanding this can help us decipher our feelings about money:

aquarius These people flourish in business when they concentrate, but they are usually more successful at making money for others than for themselves. If born into wealth, they rarely display it and seldom make use of opportunities to further their wealth. If born into poverty, they can become dishonest in money matters. The best colors for them to wear while dealing with money are electric blue or gray.

pisces People born under this sign worry greatly about their future financial security. They detest being obligated to anyone and diligently save in case there comes a time when they are no longer able to earn money. They often renege on a promise in money matters and will withdraw from an agreement despite their commitment to pay. The reason for this is that they make impulsive pledges but become anxious about their own future financial stability. They should wear mauve, purple, or lavender to enhance their money luck.

aries These people can climb the ladder of financial success quite easily, provided that they are not swayed by the flattery and ill advice of those around them. The entire purpose of their life is work and achievement, so they tend to earn money until quite late in life. They must wear any shade of red while attending meetings relating to money.

taurus These people have great business sense and often appear more affluent than they are because of their stylish dress sense and home management skills. They would do well to make financial decisions while alone, as their minds are then at their sharpest. They must wear blue when discussing money matters.

gemini Their income is always uncertain because June people lack constancy of purpose. They flit from one project to another, choosing areas where their inherent tact and eloquence help them to earn money. They should, however, persevere with one career so that their talents can raise them to the peak of success. June people who take to the wrong paths in life usually become involved in gambling or duping people with easy-money schemes. Wear silver or sparkling white to bring clean money into your life.

cancer These people worry too much about their finances and save in secret for a rainy day. They usually have financial difficulties in early life, but settle down to hard work and diligence. They can be lured into gambling by the idea of quick money, but they seldom win by speculation. They should persist with minimum-risk businesses, in which they tend to be most successful. They should wear the colors green, cream, or white.

leo These people are generally lucky in money matters and seem to obtain income from unusual and unorthodox sources. They live well, sometimes even beyond their means. They do not like being dependent on anyone financially, and if life forces these circumstances upon them, they become morose and uncommunicative. They should wear yellow, orange, pale green, or white.

virgo These people work hard and make money through persistence, rather than the brilliance of their ideas. They are materialistic and can become quite crafty or vicious in their attempts to obtain wealth. They should wear pastel colors and glossy, shiny materials.

libra These people are very intuitive and inclined to act on their first impulse. These decisions will usually be favorable. Librans are lucky in speculation and would do well to invest in stocks. They should wear blue for enhanced money luck.

scorpio These people should avoid putting things off until tomorrow, as this attitude can lead to a loss of many money-making opportunities. Scorpians generally have two or more sources of income, and they are diligent savers or investors. They also tend to repay loans quickly, not wanting the burden of debt to hang over them for long. They should wear shades of dark red or blue.

sagittarius These people are scrupulously honest about money and will even make sacrifices for the sake of honesty. Many Sagittarians who have seen poverty and ill luck will be ungenerous and petty with money. On the whole, they are worshipers of law and order and are rarely tempted to make money through illegal means. They should wear violet or mauve for financial luck.

capricorn These people do their best to become financially self-reliant very quickly, as they hate being indebted to others. Their generosity is extended to groups, rather than to individuals, and they often make charitable donations to deserving institutions. Wear gray, purple, black, or violet for special money luck.

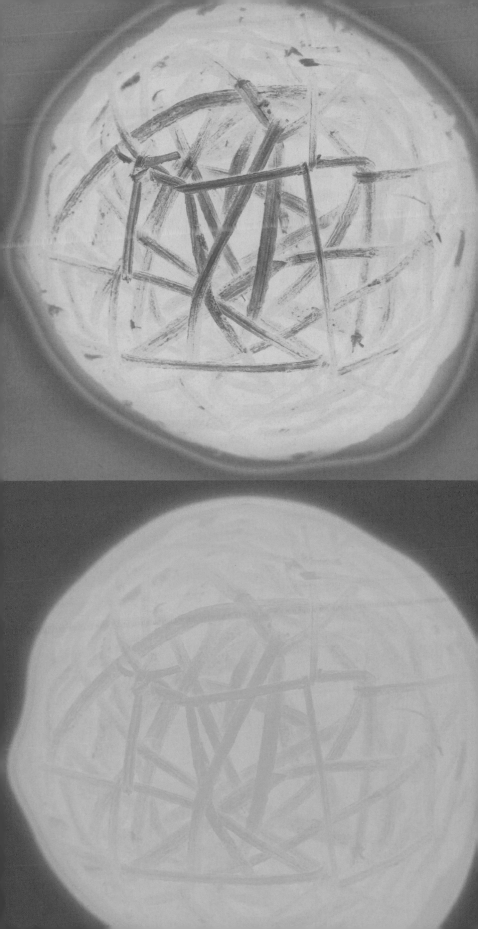

Palmistry & money

Each pair of hands is unique. The lines and mounts (the raised portions at the base of the fingers) relate to different parts of our lives and reveal what the future may hold.

Look at your fingers. If your ring finger is almost equal in length to your index finger, you are certainly interested in money, but you will try to earn it through artistic pursuits. If the ring finger is unusually long and nearly equal to the middle finger, you will still be artistic, but you will enjoy gambling and speculation. If you observe your palm, you will see the line of fate which sweeps up the hand from the wrist toward the base of the fingers, usually the middle finger (see page 57). It relates to worldly matters, such as money, career, and success:

If the line of fate arises strongly and steadily from the line of life, it shows that the person will gain wealth through hard work. If it joins the line of life low on the wrist, it denotes that in early life all income will result from employment chosen by that person's parents or relatives.

The most fortunate sign for financial success is if the line of fate arises from the wrist and climbs straight up the hand to the mount of Saturn, which lies at the base of the middle finger.

If the line starts from the mount of the Moon, near the wrist but on the opposite side to the thumb, it shows that the person's income will be dependent on his or her popularity with the general public. This is usually the case with public figures such as movie stars. If the line runs up from a woman's wrist, but is joined by a branch from the mount of the Moon on her hand, it denotes a wealthy marriage.

If the line of fate, on its way to the mount of Saturn, sends off branches to any other mount, the qualities of that mount will dominate the person's life. If the line itself goes to any mount other than the mount of Saturn, financial and career success will arise from the aspects ruled by that particular mount.

If the line of fate is abruptly cut by the line of heart, it shows that one's financial progress will be impeded by affairs of the heart. If the two lines join and proceed together, one's love life and financial status will develop together. When the line of fate is abruptly cut by the line of head, one's income is placed in jeopardy by foolish actions and decisions.

If there is a break in the line of fate there will be great financial losses in life, but if it temporarily narrows and resumes again, it indicates a changed source of income.

Career

Good fortune is not obtained without the performance of good deeds. Glory is not attained by the faithless.

Narad Puran (date unknown)

Today it is not easy to gain recognition in one's career. The workplace is highly competitive, and with the rapid development of new technologies, there is a global race to attain new skills. Furthermore, national economies are locked in competition, so that even the most highly valued positions can be lost at the drop of a few points in the exchange rate. It is becoming increasingly difficult to hold on to employment or obtain a lucrative position. Women are offered increasingly better employment opportunities as the business world unfolds before them. But the pressure of excelling at work and fulfilling the roles of mother, wife, hostess, homemaker, and investor of family finances can lead to physical and emotional exhaustion. Given this scenario, we all need a good measure of luck that will ease the rocky road of success in our chosen career. We require luck that will help us to be relatively stress free, encourage us to make quick and correct business decisions, and instill a driving ambition which can be realized only through perseverance and hard work.

Gems & career

Never take your gems for granted. They have the power to counteract negative influences and accelerate progress. This power is believed to have been absorbed by the stones while they lay underground as undiscovered minerals for millions of years. The ancient science of gemology holds that a seemingly innocuous stone can wreak havoc with your career. Conversely, wearing the correct stone can promote your desire to excel in your vocation. Follow the instructions in the first chapter for energizing your stone, so that it suits the purpose for which it is worn.

red gems Ruby, being the gem of the Sun, strengthens one's ability to command others, while improving relationships with business partners and superiors. Hessonite, a clear, dark red gem, also helps to bring success in business dealings.

orange gems Coral is ideal for people who are starting new ventures and need courage and determination. If you need to infuse fresh ideas or a burst of enthusiasm into your business projects, wearing amber will also help.

yellow gems A clear, luminous, and beautiful yellow sapphire brings not only money but also fame, honor, and a respected name. This gem also helps to focus the mind on issues at hand, promoting informed decision making. The cat's-eye protects its wearer from hidden enemies and dangers, such as undercutting and cheating in business. It also helps the wearer to liaise with government agencies to ensure a properly run business. It is widely used by people linked with the stock market and other speculative businesses.

green gems Emeralds are ideal for those of us whose career involves communication, as green improves the ability to convey one's thoughts effectively. These stones are especially helpful to writers, actors, musicians, and politicians. Known to reduce stress, they can also help people in high-powered positions. Green jade helps clarity of thought and is another good stone for people who supervise others in the workplace.

blue gems These gems inspire the qualities of creativity and responsibility. Blue sapphire is a stone that can make your career soar. It also counteracts others' envy. It is a good stone for entrepreneurs or those working in a new sector of the economy where fresh ideas are demanded. People who wear sapphires—only if the gem suits their personalities and goals—see a meteoric rise in their career.

purple gems A purple amethyst will help check anxiety and insomnia. If you are exhausted by the stress of your work and need inner calm in order to succeed, rub your forehead and temple with an energized amethyst. You will feel its soothing vibrations.

white gems White is for increased energy that flows unrestrictedly. Diamonds, eternally beautiful and with an icy fire in their depths, help the wearer to achieve name, fame, and luxury. They create the self-confidence required for making progress in one's career. Pearls enhance peace of mind and help calm busy executives who lead the jet-set life.

black gems Keep a black gem on your person to counteract the personal and professional envy of others. Stones such as jet or obsidian will absorb negative energy and clear your path toward progress and achievement.

Color & career

Which of us has never been nervous before a job interview? At one point or another, all of us have worried about what to wear or say in order to enhance our job prospects.

Until recently, work clothes were very formal in style and color. Happily, today's economy allows for a more relaxed style which can endure flexible hours of work and frequent travel. According to color therapy, colors attract negative and positive vibrations toward us, and different colors suit different situations and requirements of the working world:

red Bold red signifies action and rejuvenation, so wear this color in order to restore your energy and appear dynamic. If an entirely red outfit is too bold for your particular job, wear red accessories with dark or neutral clothing.

pink Wear this color if your job requires you to be nurturing and selfless.

orange This is a wonderful color for self-motivation. Wear orange if you are about to become self-employed or enter a new, uncharted venture.

yellow This color will enable you to communicate your thoughts more lucidly. Try to wear yellow accessories with dark clothing to appear confident and energetic.

green This color helps you make clear, logical decisions. It is rarely paired with black, as it diminishes the authority projected by this darker color.

blue Dark blue improves communication and decision-making skills. It also conveys authority and responsibility. Turquoise is a more youthful color which promotes clear thought and speech.

purple This color helps you to command respect without being overly forceful. Purple is the color of the soul, making those who wear it peaceful and calm. Lighter shades such as mauve or lilac promote relaxation.

white Wear white if you are in a position where you have to listen to the suggestions and ideas of others before taking action.

black Authority and power are the messages conveyed by this color. If you need to communicate your opinions more forcefully, black is the color for you. One should wear touches of more vibrant colors to counteract this somber color.

According to color therapy, people in certain professions flourish through the use of a particular color. While at work, you can either wear your lucky professional color or keep an object of the same shade nearby.

Accountants and people dealing with figures: blue green encourages careful analysis.

Artists, designers, creative professions: lilac for inspiration, orange for creativity.

Babysitters and children's-ward nurses: pink and green promote nurturing and compassion.

Engineers, architects, and interior designers: orange is the color of creative excellence.

Journalists, writers, public communicators: blue for inspiration, golden yellow for confident self-expression.

People who work outdoors, for example soldiers, gardeners, farmers, and many sportspeople: red for energy.

Police, guards, chefs, and herbalists: magenta, purple, and saffron for self-confidence and a calm demeanor.

Politicians, lawyers, and people in public office: royal blue and purple stand for authority and independent thinking.

Teachers, doctors, nurses, and healers: cobalt blue promotes selfless service. Also, orange, purple and their softer shades for gentleness and caring.

Symbols & career

Rudraksha bead

In the quiet, snow-encrusted foothills of the Himalayas grow row upon row of a special tree called the rudraksha tree (*Elaeocarnus ganitrus*) This tree is not particularly beautiful, as it has neither the grandeur of foliage nor the spectacle of blossom. Nevertheless, it is prized all over India for its seeds—fat, hard, round beads with an uneven, ridged surface and a color that ranges from coffee to mahogany. The seeds vary in size from that of a small peppercorn to the size of a large cherry. While the rudraksha tree is identified with Indian religious beliefs (it is considered the essence of Lord Shiva), a rudraksha seed is also believed to hold good luck properties. There are more than 123 recognized varieties of rudraksha trees all over the world, but it is only in India and Nepal that their special significance is recognized.

Each rudraksha bead is a potent symbol. A seed's governing deity, and hence its specific luck properties, is determined by the number of ridges on its shell. A single-ridged seed is extremely rare and is believed to help meditation and tranquillity. The four-ridged rudraksha is governed by the Great Bear constellation and brings financial success particularly to those in business. The twelve-ridged bead is for those who wish to gain political power, and the fourteen-ridged bead is said to bestow fame. Because of the bead's lucky properties it is used as a motif, which is printed and embroidered on fabrics. The rudraksha bead has also been proven to have bio-magnetic properties and should be worn in contact with the body. There are many fakes around, but you can recognize a genuine bead by dropping it into a glass of water; a true rudraksha will float and an imitation will sink.

215

Metals & career

People in India believe that wearing a lucky metal close to the skin or possessing an object crafted from such a metal can bring luck into one's career—I have seen friends wearing metal rings in the hope of a promotion at work. We believe that a given metal shares the qualities of its ruling planet and that these are transmitted to human beings in close contact with the metal.

gold Mars is the ruler of gold. It is a fiery and violent planet which fosters feelings of competition and ambition. Hence, this metal brings luck to those in professions that demands an aggressive nature. Wear gold to enhance competitive drive and the desire to excel in a field that is full of risks and ambitious competitors.

silver The Moon rules silver, bringing opportunities to play an important role in politics or public affairs. Wear silver if you are looking for success in a career that involves popularity or influencing people in general.

copper Burnished copper, which is a beautiful red, carries the essence of the fiery Sun. Copper can raise its wearer to a senior position in business or government. The wearer will be gifted with a strong will and a masterful authority, through which his or her career will rise.

lead This metal is governed by Mercury, the chief ruler of mankind's mental faculties. If you keep a small lead object close by, it will improve your mental agility and the retentive powers of your memory. Lead also gives you the ability to conceive of new projects.

Vastu shastra & your career

Due to the development of new technologies, as well as traffic congestion and time spent traveling to and from work, more and more people are opting to work from home. The ancient science of Vastu Shastra, which governs the principles of architecture and design, outlines the proper arrangement of our home-cum-offices:

The best direction for an office at home is the southwest. If you already have a bedroom there (as this is also the optimum direction for a bedroom), move the bedroom to the south or west portion of your home.

The owner of the business, probably yourself, should face east, north, or northeast. Chairs should be so placed that visitors face the south or west.

The receptionist or secretary should sit in the northeast corner near the entrance.

Electronic equipment, such as computers or fax machines, should be kept in the southeast corner of the office.

A table used for meetings should be in the northwest. As far as possible, staff should face the east or north.

If there is a food cabinet in the office, it should be located in the southeast corner.

A powder room is best placed in the south, west, or northwest but never in the northeast or southwest corner.

Parking facilities should be to the northeast of the home.

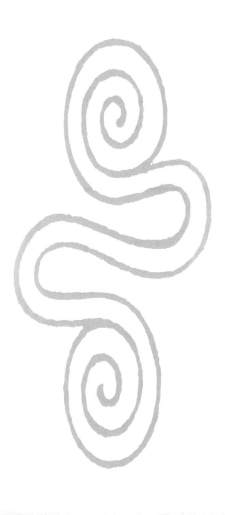

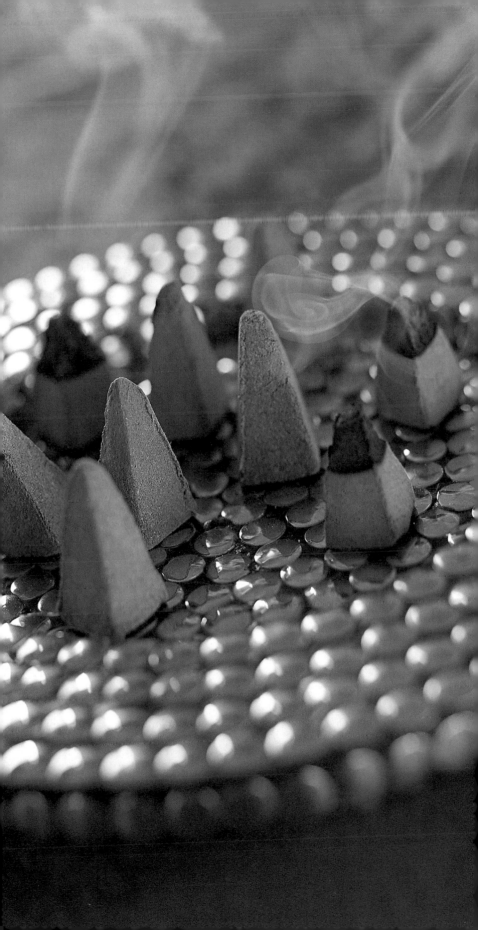

For any office, whether at home or outside, the following guidelines should be followed in conjunction with the above advice to ensure a flourishing business:

Unwanted or backdated material should be stored in the southwest corner of the basement.

The main power supply or generator used by the business should be in the southeast corner of the basement or in the southeast corner of the plot if there is no basement.

All cash will be safe in the northern part of the office, and the accounts department is best placed in the north, northeast, or east.

The staff cafeteria would be best placed in the southeastern part of the building.

Large parking lots should be on the southwest area of the plot.

Numbers & career

Your birth number affects the way in which you seek job satisfaction and prosperity. A person of one number may find a career in the stock market extremely challenging, whereas a person with a different birth number might think it too nerve-racking! Your birth number is calculated by adding together the digits of the day you were born (for example, a person born on the twenty-seventh of a month will have a birth number of nine).

number one You will wield considerable power over your colleagues and subordinates. Your career may have greater chances of success in a foreign country. The career in which you will flourish is one that requires critical analysis, research, and original thinking. Your professional advancement generally starts in your twenty-fifth year, and there will be unexpected changes in your career pattern between the ages off forty-one and forty-five. Good years for your career will be your twenty-seventh, twenty-ninth, thirty-sixth, forty-seventh, fifty-forth, sixty-third, and seventy-second. You will benefit from wearing a ruby or topaz and working in a city whose number is one and therefore in harmony with your own. Possible cities include Boston, Manchester, New York, and Sydney, and their numbers are calculated as follows (see page 40 for letter values):

B   O   S   T   O   N

2 + 7 + 3 + 4 + 7 + 5 = 28

$$2 + 8 = 10 = 1$$

number two You are hardworking and diplomatic and will rise to positions of authority. You will be most successful in a career related to education, philosophy, scientific investigation, research, or new inventions. You also do well in deals involving real estate and will benefit from business travel. Your career begins around the ages of twenty-three or twenty-four and becomes established around the age of twenty-nine, after a considerable struggle. You will probably be helped in your career by your mother or a female relative. If the numbers three, six, or nine recur in your life, you will become popular through the fine arts or politics. You often rise to the very top of your profession but cannot occupy this position for long. You tend to stabilize at second position. Wear pearl or jade for professional luck, and try to work in a city whose number is the same as your own, such as Brighton, Los Angeles, Miami, or Stockholm.

number three Your progress in your profession is slow and steady. Although your career may be interrupted, your determination will carry you on to success. You are attracted to literature and mathematics and your forty-fifth year sees an inflow of funds. You are very ambitious and love to exert your authority. Therefore, you are suited to high-ranking positions in the armed forces or government. You must be careful, however, that your dictatorial nature does not win you enemies. Wear amethyst for luck, and try to find work in a city governed by number three, such as Dublin, Lisbon, Melbourne, Moscow, or Tokyo.

number four This number is governed by Uranus, the planet of energy and movement. You can easily master several languages and should seek a career that allows you to work in the social sector. If you choose to go into some business, however, you may have to change your line of work often before finding an occupation that appeals to you. Professionally, your twentieth, twenty-second, twenty-seventh, thirty-forth, thirty-seventh, fortieth, fiftieth, and fifty-fifth years are eventful. Wear blue sapphire for luck, and look to work in a number-four city, such as London, Montreal, Stuttgart, or Washington.

number five You are a child of Mercury, and, like your planet, you are never still. You are unaffected by the lows in your career and quickly find ways to overcome difficulties. You love speculation and do well in any business that requires it. You will also excel at literary activities and accounting. Wear a diamond set in platinum or silver, and seek employment in a number-five city, such as Athens, Chicago, Dubai, Vancouver, or Vienna.

number six This number is governed by Venus, and as a consequence you are loved by all. You are extremely artistic and shine in fields such as acting, advertising, beauty, fashion, and literature. You are suitable for vocations that involve travel and meeting people. Your forty-second year marks a turning point in your career. Wear diamonds or corals for luck, and work in a number-six city, such as Cologne, Edinburgh, Oxford, Paris, or San Francisco.

number seven You have an active mind with an unquenchable thirst for knowledge. You therefore shine in research, foreign languages, or any field that requires deep and prolonged study. Possible professions include architecture, design, medicine, surgery, or town planning. Wear moonstone or pearl for luck, and try to work in a number-seven city like Hollywood or Madrid.

number eight You are a great thinker and may be interested in a career that requires technical or legal education. Computer science, engineering, mining, and real estate are other professions for which you are suited. You are generally averse to writing, but this is mainly because you are inclined to be lazy. Your thirty-seventh year is crucial in terms of your career. Wear blue sapphire, diamond, or turquoise, and work in a number eight place, such as Belfast.

number nine You are artistic and thrive on adventure and novelty. You are also analytical but tend to overwork yourself. Some professions that would suit you are engineering, travel, insurance, banking, mathematics, and research. Wear ruby, garnet, or red coral, and choose a city such as Berlin, Brussels, Rome, or Toronto in which to live and work.

Dreams & career

All of us dream, even in our waking state, of being successful and respected. While success eludes some, it appears to come effortlessly to others. Our dreams can provide answers when we are uncertain of success or the possibility of advancement in our career. They can reveal our deepest feelings, helping us to confront them.

desserts This dream foretells small returns on large investments in business.

favors To ask someone for a favor signifies a leap forward in business, whereas to grant someone a favor foretells a loss.

laboratory To see yourself in a laboratory denotes that you are chasing after a vocation in which you will not be successful. Instead, you should turn your mind to something more practical.

ladder To ascend a ladder signifies prosperity and success in a business, whereas to descend predicts failure.

potter If you see a potter, you are assured of constant and fruitful employment.

profits This is always a good dream which translates itself quite literally into life.

registration If you see yourself being registered at a hotel by someone else, it denotes that some work you have not finished will be completed by another. If you register yourself under a false name, one of your ventures is making you feel guilty and restless.

rival If you see a rival surpassing you, you will be negligent in business. If there is a rival competing against you, you will be slow in staking your claim or selling your ideas.

work To see yourself working hard denotes that you will receive the fruits of your concentrated efforts. If you see others at work, it foretells that harmonious conditions surround you. If you look for work, you will gain through unforeseen measures.

Astrology & career

A horoscope is divided into twelve houses, or sections. While the birth house and the house occupied by the Moon influence one's career, its course is determined more strongly by the tenth house. To discover the influences acting upon this portion of your horoscope, you will need to visit an astrologer. You will then be able to match the conjunction of your tenth house with the following likely occupations:

Sun   Government, Medicine, or Military

Moon   Engineer, Jeweler, Nurse, or Sailor

Mercury   Astronomy, Poet, Mathematician, or Writer

Venus   Actor, Artist, Dancer, or Interior Designer

Mars   Doctor, Soldier, Sportsman, or Surgeon

Jupiter   Judge, Lawyer, Minister, Priest, Philosopher, or Statesman

Uranus   Mathematician, Public Speaker, or Scientist

Neptune   Caterer, Hotelier, or Nurse

The planet associated with each sign of the zodiac influences the personalities of people born under it. Career luck can be enhanced if the strengths of a specific sign are built upon in order to usher in progress and prosperity. For example, an individual born to a lazy sign is unlikely to succeed in a profession that requires a twenty-four-hour working day.

The various zodiac signs, too, are suited to certain professions.

aquarius You have a scientific mind, but would also succeed in business and finance. You love public events and would be successful in events management. You are also suited to professions dealing with influencing others.

pisces You are ambitious by nature but lack the self-esteem needed to bring your dreams to fruition. The arts, music and writing are areas where you excel, but you need constant recognition. You are fond of water and the sea and would do well in shipping or other maritime professions. Foreign trade is also a suitable vocation.

aries You are a brilliant organizer and are able to lead a company or an army. You are able to chart a course of development for an organization or even a country. Your unmatched drive and ambition can carry you to the top of a career in science, journalism, or politics.

taurus You have great powers of endurance and do not tire easily. You excel in public life, and in any profession that is associated with healing or with nature.

gemini Your agile mind will carry you ahead of your rivals. You could excel as an actor, lawyer, public speaker, or lecturer. You would also do well in the stock market but must persevere with your career to become successful, as frequent changes in occupation would be detrimental.

cancer You love to speculate and would do well in business. By making the most of your vivid imagination, you would also do well as a artist, composer, or writer. Like the symbol of Cancer, the crab, you often progress in your career to a fixed point, only to stop and change course at the most crucial point. This causes great surprise among your colleagues.

leo You are a born leader and will endure the test of fire to prove it. You do well in the armed forces, finance, or public life.

virgo You love to read and would make a good reviewer of books. You would also make an effective lawyer or debater working in support of social reform. You would do well in business, but should try to combine your profession with a literary pursuit.

libra You are a devotee of learning. You would make a wonderful doctor or lawyer specializing in a particular field. Your work is governed by your sense of balance and virtue.

scorpio You have a dramatic personality that expresses itself through painting, poetry, or writing. You also have a gift for making peace between parties and could do well in government. You will become increasingly interested in spirituality or philosophy as you grow older and may even pursue a career in one of these fields.

sagittarius You change your profession often. You may move from banking to art and would do well at both. You also love music and could easily make it your profession. For your career to be successful, you must select it yourself, resisting the influence of others.

capricorn You are a natural reasoner and suited to professions that allow you to guide others and delegate authority. You would do well in government.

Palmistry & career

The lines and mounts of the hand can be read to reveal how we feel about our career and respond to the opportunities it presents. First, look at the mount of the Sun, which lies at the base of your ring finger. If it is prominent, you will be successful and well known. If it is weak, you may still succeed in business and finance but will labor more for the benefit of others than for yourself. The length of the fingers also tells a story. If the index finger is very long, it denotes an inclination toward a strident form of politics or religion. When the little finger is long and almost reaches the nail of the ring finger, the person will be gifted at verbal self-expression, and he or she will excel in a related profession.

The line of fate, which provides the biggest clue to the future of your career:

If the line of fate ascends to the mount of Jupiter, at the base of the index finger, your energy and determination will take you to the pinnacle of power.

If a branch from the line of fate grows toward the Mount of Jupiter, success will come to you at that point in life.

If this line goes toward the finger of Saturn (middle finger), it is not a good omen, as there will be a setback in the person's career.

When the line of fate rises from the line of head, success will come late in life and after much struggle.

When the line is broken or irregular, the career will be a roller-coaster ride of successes and failures.

If there is a complete break in the line, it is a sign that your career will come to an end.

Twin lines of fate denotes two distinct careers that the person will follow. This is even more true if the two lines lead to different mounts.

People without a line of fate are often successful but seem unaffected by their success.

To learn more about the future of your career, look at the line of Sun, also called the line of Apollo or the line of success. It begins anywhere low on the palm and extends to the mount of the Sun, which is located under the third or ring finger (see page 60). This line increases the success indicated by a good fate line.

When this line arises from the line of life, it denotes success in an artistic career. If the line of head is simultaneously sloping, a career in writing or another imaginative field is foretold.

Many lines on the mount of Sun show a highly artistic nature, but too many ideas crowd the mind and hamper success.

An absence of the line of Sun denotes that in spite of rigorous hard work and determination, the person will never achieve success and honor.

When the line of Sun is juxtaposed with a fairly straight line of head, the person does all he or she can to attain wealth and power.

Happiness

*O Wise Man ! As in the transit of waters, the earth is not shaken,
so should you not feel shattered when miseries affect you.*
Rig-Veda (between 1500 and 900 B.C.)

What is true happiness? Is it a new car, a better job or a good-
looking partner? What is sorrow? Is it the lack of material wealth,
unemployment, or being alone? If this were the case, the definitions of
happiness and sadness would be simple. But they are not. In fact it would
be true to say that half the confusion in the world comes from not
understanding how little we truly need to make us happy. A person who
is liberated and at peace is not disturbed by the fluctuations of happiness
and sadness that are an essential part of human life. He is happy in his
heart and finds paradise within himself. In our lifetimes, we will all chase
an illusory rainbow of happiness. Instead, we should look for the seed of
joy deep within our souls. This is the seed of permanence in an ever-
changing world, a seed that can flower into a beautiful lotus, untouched
by anger, dishonesty, envy, greed, and wickedness that surround us. In a
world that is transient and impermanent, this alone is true happiness.

Gems & happiness

Many of us love to wear dazzling gems that shine with a pure and lustrous fire. When these jewels bring us happiness in other areas of our life, we are doubly rewarded. Gems of different colors can rectify a person's color deficiencies and related character failings.

red gems Wear rubies if you are stressed or unsettled. This ambassador of the sun brings vitality and rejuvenation, helping one bask in the warmth of self-fulfillment. Pink stones, such as rose quartz, also calm the soul and bring appreciation for all that is positive in life.

orange gems Indian women and children are often seen wearing fat, burnt-orange coral beads. Coral safeguards our emotional well-being, bringing calm and mental stability.

yellow gems Golden yellow gems, such as topaz, citrine, or yellow sapphire, help us to overcome mental and physical exhaustion. Ruled by Jupiter, who also controls the life force within the human body, these stones create balance between the forces operating within us.

green gems Heal yourself of jealousy and low self-esteem by wearing an emerald or jade. Green is the color of harmony, and these stones will promote calmness in your life.

blue gems This is the color of the element of air—during storms the sky can turn a violent blue or indigo. Specifically, sapphire is ruled by Saturn, which also controls the nervous system. However, all blue gems promote tranquillity, bringing joy to your life and the lives of those around you.

purple gems This is the color of spirituality, which is the ultimate happiness. Amethyst controls fear and anxiety and helps one develop faith in a power beyond the material world.

white gems Diamonds and pearls stand for purity and confidence. Wear them during low points in your life in order to boost your courage and sense of self-worth.

Navagraha gems

Each planet influences our lives to some degree. Indians worship nine planets, collectively known as the *navagraha*, which together ensure our health, wealth and happiness. Through the ages the *navagraha* has been explored in depth. Sanskrit texts talk of Mercury as a cloudy, blue bud. They also describe the golden complexion of Jupiter and the red countenance of Mars, which is as brilliant as lightning.

The nine planetary stones, namely ruby, pearl, coral, emerald, yellow sapphire, diamond, blue sapphire, garnet, and cat's-eye, can be set in gold and crafted into a single piece of jewelery. Encrusted with *navaratna*, or nine gems, this sumptuous ornament will bring every form of luck to its wearer. For this reason, *navaratna* rings, necklaces, earrings, and lockets are very popular throughout India.

Color & happiness

Color therapy addresses the unique relationship between color and emotion. The colors that you choose to wear or are repeatedly attracted to indicate your idea of happiness. Similarly, colors you dislike can hint at issues you ought to address in order to be happier and more at peace with yourself. An informed use of color can make our lives more rewarding and our souls more content.

red If you are drawn to this color, you love to be the center of attention and can be somewhat insensitive to the feelings of those around you. You are happiest when involved in exciting situations. If you dislike red, you are probably afraid of rejection or defeat. You need to overcome this fear and try to put red energy back into your life.

pink People who favor this color are loving and sensitive by nature. However, they depend on emotional support from others and, for their own sake, should gain more self-confidence. If you dislike pink, you may be burdened by negative feelings toward your mother or father, and you need to come to terms with these.

orange or peach If you like these colors, you are probably determined, energetic, and happiest when active. Dislike of these colors could indicate that you are suffering from mental or physical exhaustion.

yellow If you like yellow, you are happiest when surrounded by happy, lively people. If you shun yellow, you are probably suffering from a feeling of helplessness.

green People who like this color are most at peace when able to observe others without becoming too involved. They conceal strong emotions and appear detached. If this sounds familiar, try wearing a touch of yellow to help you communicate your feelings. If you dislike green, you have probably experienced loneliness or disappointment at some point in you life.

blue If you like blue, you enjoy either working independently or taking the lead. You need to find time to relax and recharge yourself. If you dislike blue, you probably have a deep-rooted fear of losing your position or honor.

purple If attracted to purple, you are most tranquil when surrounded by thinking people whose ideas excite you and whose characters you admire. However, you need to learn to listen to others and forgive their faults. If you are averse to purple, it shows that you are feeling restricted by someone's hold over you, or you are suffering from blocked creativity.

white When you wear white, you reveal that you enjoy simplicity but also like to be noticed. When you are repelled by white, you may fear being parted from a loved one.

black This color suggests that you are in control, but it could also be used to mask a feeling of low self-esteem. If you avoid black, this could mean that there is a block in your leadership energy that needs to be addressed.

Symbols & happiness

Indians love decoration and will seize any opportunity to add design, color, and detail to their surroundings. Hindus wear a *bindi*, or a dot, on the forehead, as a mark of good fortune, fashioning it into a work of art with various colors and shapes. Married women adorn their necks with a marriage necklace called a *mangalsutra*, which is one of the essential symbols of a happy life.

poorna kumbha Throughout history humans have yearned to conquer death. Indian mythology contains stories of sages who spent years doing penance in their quest for immortality. While physical immortality and permanent youth remained a fantasy, early Indian thinkers pondered about how to achieve the fullest experience possible, believing that a rich life brings us as close as possible to the dream of eternal life. This belief is embodied in the symbol of the *poorna kumbha*, a pot with mango leaves and a coconut on top. *Poorna kumbha* is used to decorate everything from trucks to wedding invitations.

coconut The coconut also symbolizes the fullness of life and is called a *kalpavriksha*, or giver of rewards. This is because each part of the tree is useful. With its hard exterior and soft, liquid center, the coconut is used to represent life as a combination of strength and fluidity, resilience and purity, and as being full of generosity and richness. The coconut is displayed in many Indian homes, due to its ability to promote luck and happiness. To honor older people, it is presented to them as a gift.

amulets In ancient times, man's worship of the elements and his ancestors developed into a mystic pantheism, in which men and women sought to appease the forces that controlled their material and spiritual destiny. This included the fashioning of lucky amulets, whose shape and design were believed to counteract negative forces and bring happiness into one's life. Amulets were worn on the body, sometimes in view and sometimes concealed within the folds of a scarf or kerchief. The first reference to this practice appears in an ancient text dating back to the first millennium B.C. Amulets are still considered very lucky and are said to bring certain happiness. There are specific amulets for different purposes and age groups made from a variety of materials and often bearing the following patterns:

tiger claws These are fashioned into a locket in the belief that the wearer will imbibe some of the strength of the animal and be able to face life bravely. Because tiger hunting is now banned in India, glass, gold, and gems are fashioned in the shape of tiger claws.

containers Tiny, replica containers are worn as lockets. A few grains or a slip of paper decorated with a chart, charm, or verse are placed inside in order to ensure fertility. These boxes are usually cylindrical but can also be round, square, or oval in shape. They are embellished with mystical motifs or religious inscriptions.

Vastu shastra & happiness

One means of ensuring that happiness resides in a home is the ritual of Grah Pravesh, or the entering of a new home. Vastu Shastra discourages people from moving into an unfinished home where only a few rooms are habitable, as missing doors, roofs, and walls are extremely inauspicious. For a newly built home, any day except Tuesday is considered fortunate for Grah Pravesh. According to Vastu Shastra, the most auspicious months are January, February, April, and May. For moving into a previously owned home, the months of February, March, April, May, July, November, and December are believed to be most favorable. All days of the week except Sunday and Tuesday are likely to bring happiness and prosperity. It is always best to move in during the day, as nighttime is inauspicious.

It is customary to decorate a new home with flowers and light a lamp to attract luck into the home. Most Indians also heat a cupful of milk and allow it to boil over in a ceremony that symbolizes a surfeit of happiness and good fortune in their new home. Prayers are said, and divine blessings are invoked to ensure peace and progress. It is important that a new home be occupied immediately after Grah Pravesh; otherwise the positive effects of this ritual will be dispelled.

Numbers & happiness

When our relationships are harmonious, happiness follows, but when there is a clash of personalities, nothing seems to go right. Numerology can tell us how to bring happiness into our lives through positive interaction with other people. Calculate your birth number by adding together the digits of the day you were born (for example, a person born on the twenty-seventh of any month will have a birth number of nine).

The qualities attached to specific birth numbers create affinity between individuals:

1	1, 3, 6
2	1, 7
3	3, 6, 9
4	4, 1, 2, 7, 8
5	all numbers, especially 5
6	3, 6, 9
7	2
8	4
9	3, 6, 9

Just as we warm to certain people, other people trigger either lack of interest or dislike. Numerology can predict such snap judgments and the outcome of relationships. For example, when two number eights form a relationship, one person sacrifices himself emotionally or physically for the other. Further, number six people invariably disagree with number ones, and when number nines associate with number eights they enhance their own fatalistic tendencies.

There are other tenets of numerology that we should bear in mind in our search for happiness:

People with the birth numbers one, two, or six and a spiritual number of six are blessed with good fortune.

People with a birth number six and a spiritual number of nine will reap more happiness than they have earned.

A series of ascending numbers is more fortunate than a descending one. For example the house number 579 will be luckier than 631.

If a number is repeated three or four times in a birth date, it denotes a life full of luxury and good luck. A person born on the first of November will be extremely lucky, because one is the number of power and glory.

The appearance of one or two zeros in a birth date enhances a person's ability to bear hardship and sorrow, as they achieve wisdom through the years.

Dreams & happiness

Happiness is the ultimate gift that we hope for. When we are utterly content and at peace, we sleep more soundly and are less able to recollect our dreams. In the final analysis, it is this restful, restoring, and seemingly dreamless sleep that we all crave. There are many secrets hidden in our dreams about the happiness or sorrow in store for us.

arrow To see an arrow signifies that celebrations or pleasurable journeys will follow.

basket A full basket denotes limitless success and happiness.

cage A cage full of birds signifies wealth and beautiful children. One bird denotes personal happiness. A caged wild animal shows that you will overcome your troubles.

doves To see doves indicates that peace and joy will be your soul mates.

ecstasy To dream of being ecstatic shows that a loved, long-absent friend will fill your soul.

gift To see yourself receiving a gift means that you will suddenly become very fortunate.

merriment To see yourself merry indicates that your plans will be fruitful.

rhinestones To dream of rhinestones indicates that pleasures will be temporary or short-lived, although diamonds reveal that sudden good luck can be expected.

running If you see yourself running with others, it denotes the successful completion of a project. Running alone can mean that you will outstrip your colleagues, experience loss, or fall into a depression.

valley A green and fruitful valley is evidence of joy to come.

wine To dream of drinking wine foretells good times to come. To see barrels of wine indicates great luxury.

Astrology & happiness

The signs of the zodiac have very little to do with our definitions of happiness. However, according to Indian astrology, there is an auspicious moment for every event to take place, which will ensure its success and invite luck into one's life. In India, the timing of events is governed by the Moon. The fourteen days of the waxing Moon are considered especially auspicious. Each day of waxing toward a full Moon brings a greater degree of artistic feeling into the character of a newborn child, and a child born on the day of a full Moon is very lucky indeed; many Indian seers and sages were born on a full-Moon day.

More than most people, Indians watch the Moon and its effects on human life. The human body is composed largely of water, and Indians believe that the Moon influences the forces in the body as it does the tides of the ocean. In comparison to the full Moon, which is when most Indian festivals are celebrated, the new Moon is less important. The exception to this rule is the festival of lights, called *Diwali*. This is considered the darkest night of the year, and rows of tiny oil lamps are lit to symbolically dispel the darkness of ignorance and avarice. Astronomers and geophysicists claim that this night, when the Moon is not seen at all, is heavily charged with magnetic activity. At this time of year the new Moon is considered fortunate and auspicious, but there is also a popular belief that on the new-Moon day, negative forces are at their strongest. Construction and quarry workers, whose jobs are hazardous, do not work on new-Moon days. Pregnant women, babies, and children are also kept indoors.

Muhurta or auspicious days and times

Indian astrology provides a set of auspicious times, or *muhurtas,* for starting or conducting activities and events. Traditionally, a *muhurta* lasts forty-eight minutes and can occur at any time during the day. Each year, various *muhurtas* are identified by astrologers and recorded in an almanac called a *panchang* which is published on New Year's Day. In some communities, reading out of a *panchang* on the first day of the new year is a grand social event.

Many Indians identify the *muhurta* for every important activity they embark upon. This could be marriage, starting a new venture, undertaking a journey, or signing vital documents. Some people look for well-established, traditional *muhurtas* which are considered universally auspicious. These occur on four days of each year:

The first day of the waxing Moon in the Hindu month of Chaitra or March, also called Gudi Padva.

The third day of the waxing Moon in the Hindu month of Vaishakh, or the latter half of April, also called Akshay Trittiya.

The tenth day of the bright half of the Hindu month of Ashwin, or late October, which is also the festival of Dussehra.

The first day in the bright half of the Hindu month Kartik, or November, after Diwali.

In a pastoral society, the sun brings its own *muhurtas.* The Brahma Muhurta, considered auspicious, energizing, and beautiful, is the first hint of dawn, when hues of mango and watermelon begin to suffuse the horizon. This is the time to experience nature's silence combining with the peace of your soul. Another lucky time is called Godhuli, literally meaning the cloud of dust raised by the hooves of cattle returning home at eventide.

Intuitions and vibrations

The Hindu text *The Bhagavad Gita* describes how the knowledge of life, as taught by Lord Krishna, was revealed to the warrior Arjuna, who was destined to hear it. Indians are strong believers in the existence of lucky people who bring good fortune into the lives of others. How does one find those bearers of serendipity? This can be done by sharpening one's intuition, so that we recognize the positive and negative vibrations emanating from other people toward ourselves. Many people do this instinctively: they are repelled by one person but attracted to another.

Meeting the right person at the right time can change your entire life, but there is another ingredient in the secret recipe for success. One should also have the wisdom to recognize an opportunity and seize it with both hands. To do this, one needs to be completely openminded, free of self-pride, and hardworking. A closed mind and the feeling that one knows best can be the undoing of potentially lucky people. We all need to look for the good fortune that invariably comes our way. We have to teach ourselves to recognize the vibrations sent out by people, places, and circumstances, so that all the good things that destiny has in store will not be lost through a moment's apathy or self-absorption.

Let us learn to seek out good fortune by becoming lucky, capable, happy, and giving individuals who carry an aura of peace, happiness, and generosity which touches other people wherever we go.

Luck out of your hands

O incoming and outgoing breath !
Save me from the fears of death.

Atharva-Veda (date unknown)

There are times in everyone's life when, no matter how hard we try, something that we desperately want does not materialize. You may wear all the gems that you possess, chant every lucky verse, or match your birth number with every other number in your life, but success still seems elusive. This is what Indians term *kismet, bhagya*, destiny or "luck out of your hands." This last phrase encapsulates the belief that each person is born with a set of rules to which his or her life will largely adhere. Only a great effort or a sudden influence, from inside or outside the individual, can alter these guiding principles. Closely linked to this belief is the Hindu philosophy of karma, which is a cosmic law of cause and effect. Thus, there are two aspects that determine our personal destiny: one's innate human nature and action, which includes evasive and unintentional action.

Karmic destiny is the result of a person's thoughts, feelings, desires, and actions, all with consequences that are only partially visible. We keep rotating within the ever-turning wheel of birth, death, and rebirth, while playing out our destiny and accumulating more karma. Karma is therefore seen as a celestial law of debit and credit whereby each person achieves points for good or evil. Karma balances the books by transporting the individual through lifetime after lifetime.

The only way to improve one's destiny at the most fundamental level is to build good karma through each thought, word, and action. Only then can we begin to realize the fruits of fortune in our present lives.

Death

We all want to know how we can improve our lives, but no one likes to think about death. The only enduring fact about life is that death is inevitable; a life well lived and a life devoted to falsehood and wickedness will both end in death. No amount of luck tools, worn, chanted, painted, or divined, can alter this simple truth. Endeavor to lead a good and full life replete with joy, love, and compassion. While making this your first priority, you should always invite luck into your life and learn to live with the bad times. Nothing in life is permanent—what glows bright and pure today will be snuffed out tomorrow.

I end this book with a story that I would like to share with you.

Once upon a time, there was a king who lived in a beautiful vanilla-and-gold palace in a city paved with precious gems. He was very happy with his wife and children and ruled his subjects well. Soon, he found that his wealth was beginning to dwindle, his kingdom began to lessen in magnificence, and his wife became unhappy and bitter. He could find no reason for this.

The king went to visit a sage on the outskirts of his capital. The sage welcomed him and gave him a sealed earthen pot, saying that it contained the magic of luck and success. The king was overjoyed and, bowing low to the sage, made his way back to the palace. Excited at the prospect of finding a secret charm or potion, he took the pot to his chamber and opened it, but all he saw within was a neatly folded scrap of paper. Intrigued, he lifted it out and read the four words it bore: "This too shall pass." The king pondered the meaning of the message and vowed to overcome his misfortune by working hard toward his goal and maintaining a positive attitude.

Soon his fortunes reversed, and he was back at the height of his glory. One day, the same sage came to his palace. The king received him with full honor and asked him the purpose of his visit. "I forgot to mention the entire secret regarding the pot the last time I saw you," answered the sage. The king was confused. After all, what more could he ask for? The sage continued, "You are to open the pot and read the message again. I meant for you to learn its secret when you are at your lowest and your highest. You are a mighty and wealthy king now, but, Your Majesty, unfortunately this too shall pass."

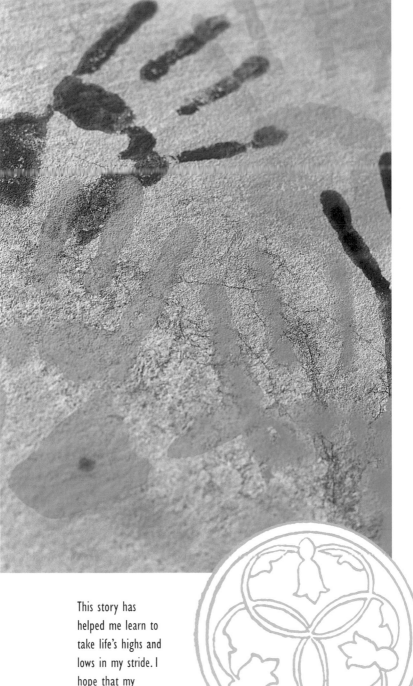

This story has
helped me learn to
take life's highs and
lows in my stride. I
hope that my
readers are inspired to
enrich their lives and
then to look beyond, to the
realm of what is permanent
and everlasting. Three things that will
never change are truth, goodness, and faith. These alone form the
foundation of eternal luck.

Bibliography

Aurobindo, Shri *The Upanishads*, Sri Aurobindo Ashram, 1971

Baba, Bangali *The Yogasutra of Patanjali*, Motilal Banarasidass, 1996

Cheiro *The Cheiro Book of Fate and Fortune*, Barrie and Jenkins 1971

Bharadwaj, Monisha *Inside India*, Kyle Cathie, 1998

Bhattacharya, Dr. Benoytosh *Gem Therapy*, Firma

Bloomfield, M. *Hymns of the Atharva-Veda*, Motilal Banarasidass, 1977–1996

Chazzari, Suzy *Color*, Element Books, 1998

Deb, S. R. *The Chakras of the Human Body*, 1921

Devi, Shakuntala *Astrology For You*, Orient Paperbacks, 1983

Goel, B. S. *Third eye and Kundalini*, Third Eye Foundation of India, 1985

Griswold, H. D. *The Religion of the Rig Veda*, Motilal Banarasidass, 1999

Hindman Miller, Gustavus *The Dictionary of Dreams*, Prentice-Hall, 1984

Hindu World, Vol. 1 and 2, Benjamin Walker, Indus, 1995

Iyer, L. *Handbook of Precious Stones*, Calcutta, 1948; Kaviratna *Charaka Samhita*, 1899

Kutumbiah, P. *Ancient Indian Medicine*, Madras, 1962

Patil, Vimla *Celebrations*, India Book House, 1994

Raman, B. V. *Notable Horoscopes*, Motilal Banarasidass, 1981

Raman, Prof V. V. *Principles and Practice of Vastu Shastra*, Vidya Bhavan, 1996

Rao, R. G. *Your Fortune From Thy House*, Sagar Publications, 1995

Ray, P. C. *A History of Hindu Chemistry*, Calcutta, 1907

Sharma, Jagdish *Bhartiya Vastugyan*, Vidya Bhavan, 1996

Shastri, J. L. *The Garud Purana*, Motilal Banarasidass, 1987–1995

Tulli, Mahan Vir *Your Future Through Astro-Numerology*, Sagar Publications, 1992

Tripathi, Dr. R. P. *Mantra Sagar*, Jyotish Prakashan, 1996

Index